SAVING AMERICA'S REAL ESTATE

Restoring Accountability and Transparency
to Real Estate Conveyance in America

I. MERS: Why So Much Confusion?
II. How to Clean up MERS
III. Abolish the Bearer Note
IV. Abolish Foreclosure Reversal
V. Understanding MERS Litigation: A Title Analysis

By

DAVID HOSTYK

TABLE OF CONTENTS

DISCLAIMER

Nothing in this book should be considered legal advice. If you are involved in a foreclosure action, please seek competent legal advice immediately.

STYLE NOTE: When the word "holder" is capitalized (i.e. "Holder"), the word is being used according to UCC paragraph 3 to mean the party in possession of a note that is endorsed to the party in possession or in blank (to bearer).

INTRODUCTION

The modernization of real estate conveyance has produced both speed and efficiency, but at the price of decreased transparency and accountability. One of the main culprits is MERS, not because there is anything wrong with its theoretical model, but because of its muddy and cumbersome business model. The lack of transparency is so acute, that MERS has been involved in litigation in every state, if not every county of the country, in both State and Federal courts.

In the accompanying book, "MERS, Notes, and Mortgages, a Title Analysis", we deconstruct the components of debt ownership, into title, equity, servicing and custodianship. We show that MERS only operates in the dimension of title, and only in terms of the mortgage. A matrix is then constructed showing the relationships of the component parts of MERS, notes and mortgages. In Chapter 1 of this book we analyze why so many lawyers, judges, journalists, professors and economists are confused about this subject. The confusion emanates from four different failures: poor use of words, the misuse of legal fictions, lack of transparency through poor execution, and the mixing of law and title. In Chapter 2, the MERS business model is analyzed and suggestions are made as to how MERS should be reformed. Finally, in Chapter 5, the three waves of litigation involving MERS are analyzed and explained; and the various outcomes are explained in both legal and economic terms.

Along the way, two other topics are discussed since both are aggravated by MERS' obtuseness, and both issues contribute to the chaotic situation. The first issue is the continued confusion caused by the bearer note. In Chapter 3 the history of paper as a store of value is reviewed, from its ancient beginnings to its current demise; and I explain why I believe that the bearer note should be abolished. Another sensitive topic is foreclosure reversal due to lender fraud. In Chapter 4, I explain why I believe that foreclosure reversal is harmful and can be replaced by a regime of penalties against misbehaving lenders.

MERS is not a conspiracy to defraud America. MERS was formed to serve a valuable economic function and it actually authored a brilliant solution in the realm of title. Its model is not based on fraud or any of the other criminal activities which it is accused of perpetrating. "MERS, Notes, and Mortgages" showed the beauty and usefulness of MERS' title model. In this book we show how and where MERS went wrong, and how to fix it.

I. MERS: WHY SO MUCH CONFUSION?

Across the United States, people are confused about MERS (Mortgage Electronic Registration Systems). Lawyers are confused about MERS. Economists and journalists are confused about MERS. Law Professors and State Supreme Court Justices are confused about MERS. Even MERS is confused about MERS. The confusion runs wide, and it runs deep, from coast to coast. Indeed, in the history of the United States, did any other entity, or issue, ever generate litigation in all fifty states, in both state and federal courts? And was there any other issue in which so many people got it wrong? Here are just a few examples of the immense confusion out there. (Each of these cases is discussed in "A Title Analysis of MERS Litigation" below. *For citations, see Appendix C.*)

1) A federal judge in North Dakota wrote the following in *Bray vs. Bank of America et al* (p. 10): ".....MERS' possession of the note would give it ownership of the mortgage. The Court finds as a matter of law that MERS owns both the note and the mortgage and thus can foreclose on the real property in question." In these two sentences, the honorable judge made at least five mistakes. (HINT: MERS can never own the note.)

2) A Florida Court of Appeals, in *Taylor v. Deutsche Bank* wrote the following (p. 7) "...the mortgage document....grants to MERS the status of a non-holder in possession....". That, is impossible. (MERS in this case was never in physical or constructive possession of the note).

3) An Alabama Appeals Court, in the case *Crum v. LaSalle* states that MERS has authority to do anything the lender can do "... including selling the note...". That, is impossible. (HINT: MERS neither buys nor sells notes).

4) The Missouri Court of Appeals in *Bellistri v. Ocwen Loan Servicing, LLC* decided that since MERS claimed to have assigned the note to plaintiff, and clearly didn't, the plaintiff did not have the right to foreclose. The honorable court made at least five mistakes. (HINT: Notes are negotiated through payment, endorsement, and delivery; not through an Assignment of Mortgage executed weeks, months, or years later).

5) The U.S. District Court of Nevada, in *Smith vs. Community Lending, Inc.* states that "In fact, MERS does not hold legal title despite the language of the First Deed-of-trust". This sentence contains multiple mistakes.

6) A Congressman on the radio program Marketplace states that MERS bifurcates the mortgage from the note. Not true. (HINT: MERS separates the title of the mortgage from the equity of the mortgage. It does not separate the equity of the mortgage from the equity of the note.)

7) Thousands (maybe millions?) of Satisfactions of Mortgage across the country state that MERS has received full payment of the mortgage. False. (HINT: MERS never touches the money).

8) In many cases around the country, lawyers for lenders who brought foreclosure actions in the name of MERS, made absurd and incorrect assertions. In the Arkansas case *MERS v. Southwest Homes of Arkansas*, the Judge writes: "MERS asserts

that it held legal title to the property..." Wrong. If lawyers for plaintiff made that assertion, they don't understand the material. (Did they really claim that, or did the judge misunderstand their argument?)

These are just a few of the many ridiculous, absurd, and nonsensical statements about MERS made by bloggers, lawyers, judges, journalists and economists. In response to this confusion, I created an Internet site www.mersnews.com. The Internet site contains a Tutorial about MERS which covers some of the material we cover here. In addition, I have posted all critical court cases concerning MERS so that it is available in one location and they are sorted by state. The full text of these cases, where available, has been uploaded.

But I felt the need to sort out the various issues in a more systematic fashion. So I wrote two books: this book of essays and a companion book "MERS, Notes, and Mortgages" which is a tutorial explaining the Title mechanics of debt ownership and negotiability.

MERS was created in 1994 to solve a nagging problem delaying the efficient workings of the market. The problem was that notes can be traded in minutes, or even seconds. Yet the recording of the assignment of the security instrument guaranteeing those notes can take weeks, or even months to show up in the Public Records due to the lack of resources available to many Clerks of Court. MERS solves this problem very efficiently and contributes positively towards making the markets more efficient.

MERS was pretty unknown to the public for its first few years of existence. But as the foreclosure crisis developed, snowballed, and then swamped the country, MERS came into the national limelight. First of all, MERS had to be named in many cases since they held title to second mortgages which needed to be wiped out by the Holder of the first loan. Secondly, assignments of mortgages that had been executed by MERS became suspect. These documents were signed by something never seen before, a "certified vice president", or a "certified secretary" of MERS. Nobody understood what that meant. More surprising, there turned out to be 25,000, or more of these so called certified officers. Even when executed correctly, the legitimacy of these assignments was a source of legal debate. But hundreds of thousands of instruments were clearly not drafted correctly or executed correctly. And that's besides the robo-signing which affected MERS' documents. Finally, and most importantly, MERS - until July 22, 2011 – engaged in two different legal fictions. First, the Holder of a note could bring a foreclosure action using the name of MERS. The consequence was that an untold number of borrowers were being sued by an entity whose name, and existence, were unknown to them. Secondly, if the lender so desired, it could transfer possession of an endorsed note to those "certified officers" so that MERS could purport to be the Holder of the note. In sum, the public saw that MERS was bringing foreclosure actions across the country; and executing suspect documents with suspect procedures. Naturally, MERS became a target of multiple lawsuits that claimed that MERS did not have the right to assign mortgages, or to satisfy mortgages, or to foreclose on mortgages.

Actually, three waves of litigation hit MERS during the first decade of the century. The first wave concerns the legitimacy of assignments of mortgages executed by MERS. Secondly, in parallel - and often in the same lawsuits – MERS' standing as plaintiff in a foreclosure action was challenged. Opponents of MERS asked how MERS could be the owner of a mortgage, and the agent of the lender, at the same time. Good question (which we will answer). Another main line of attack was questioning how MERS could ever be the mortgagee (of a mortgage) or the beneficiary (of a deed-of trust). Isn't the lender always the mortgagee, or the beneficiary, as the case may be? In addition, how can MERS bring a foreclosure action if it is not the Holder of the note? The third wave of litigation was initiated by various Clerks of Court who challenged the essence of MERS - which is to act as a registry for mortgages nationwide. Isn't it the duty of the Clerk of Court to record assignments? Isn't it in the interest of the nation for this information to be public and not privatized by special interest groups? All of these questions are answered in the chapter "A Title Analysis of MERS Litigation". In that section, we analyze the various issues, review how they were resolved in the different states, summarize the outcome of these waves of litigation, and offer an economic explanation of the results.

But first we have to analyze the title components of notes, mortgages and MERS. Why? Because **MERS is a problem in Title**. MERS exists first, in the realm of title. Without clearly defining the title components of notes and mortgages, it is impossible to understand the real interest that MERS has in real estate. This analysis can be found in the accompanying book, "MERS, Notes, and Mortgages", which is a 17 part tutorial. That Tutorial explains the component parts of notes and mortgages. That book also explains the many distinctions that have to be made, which are not well understood:

1) Note vs. mortgage
2) Mortgage vs. deed-of-trust
3) Mortgagee vs. mortgagor
4) Title-Theory vs. Lien-Theory
5) Ownership in title vs. ownership in equity
6) Holder vs. owner vs. servicer
7) Initial conditions for foreclosure v. final conditions
8) Do notes follow the mortgage or do mortgages follow the note?

Finally, "MERS, Notes, and Mortgages" builds a matrix of relationships between all of the above and MERS.

But why is this necessary? Why not go straight to the cases and see how the lawyers and judges of the land handled these issues? Aren't they the parties most qualified to handle these issues? No. On the contrary: Title is not law. Title is not a branch of the law. In fact, title is not taught in law school. Title is not even practiced by lawyers in many states; some states actually prohibit transactional lawyers from engaging in title examination and the sale of title insurance. Despite impressions to the contrary, practitioners of law are not necessarily well versed in title.

1. Title is not Law

And this is the first answer to the question: Why is there so much confusion about MERS?

There is so much confusion about MERS because "Title" is not law. "Title" is a practice very much apart from the practice of law. Title is not taught in law school and most lawyers are not fluent in the ways of Title.

It is telling, and interesting, to note that practitioners of law and practitioners of title use the term "Title" to mean different things. To a lawyer, "title" means ownership. Lawyers divide ownership into two domains: 1) public information concerning ownership is called "legal title" and 2) beneficial ownership is called "equitable title". To a title practitioner, public information concerning owner- ship is simply "title" and is the same as "legal title". And to a title practitioner there is no such thing as "equitable title". A practitioner of title is often not able to determine equitable ownership, espe- cially when the relevant documents are not in the public record. And besides, why would a practitioner of title be concerned with equitable ownership?

Definition of:	To a practitioners of Law	To a practitioners of Title
"title"	Ownership	Publicly known Owner
"legal title"	Publicly known Owner	Publicly known Owner
"equitable title"	Beneficial Owner	**Contradiction of terms**

While there are many lawyers that are learned in Title – it is not because they went to law school. The reason that they are learned in title is that they work in title. The only way to know title is to practice title and most lawyers do not practice title. Yet that didn't stop endless pronouncements by lawyers and judges concerning MERS even though MERS is a problem in title before it is a problem in law. Judges, learned judges, brilliant judges, added to the noise by deciding cases about MERS when they were not really well versed in title. Hence all the mistakes quoted above – which really are only the tip of the iceberg.

Am I being disrespectful to the legal profession? Not in the least. No one would think twice if I said that I don't go to court for surgery. Or to fix my computer. Or to wire my house. It's obvious that surgery, computers, and electricity are not taught in law school. What the public doesn't know (and what lawyers do not admit) is that Title is also not taught in law school. Judges and lawyers are not necessarily qualified to examine, search, or clear title. Yet those same judges had the final word on MERS in countless cases

2. Sloppy Wordmanship

There is one court decision which stands out above all the rest for correct analysis, clear writing, and clarity of thought. That is the decision by the Minnesota Supreme Court in *Jackson v. MERS*. I devote a chapter to this case because *Jackson* hit the nail on the head. And if every judge who wrote incorrectly about MERS had read *Jackson* (and/or "MERS, Notes and Mortgages") they would not have erred so grievously. The court in *Jackson* not only understood the issues, they thought clearly and wrote clearly. This is the second answer. **2. There is so much confusion about MERS because of sloppy thinking due to the blurring of definitions and the misuse of words**.

As George Orwell pointed out so often – you cannot think clearly if you don't use words clearly. In his essay "Politics and the English Language", he wrote about the English language:

"It becomes ugly and inaccurate because our thoughts are foolish, but **the slovenliness of our language makes it easier for us to have foolish thoughts**".

And MERS is guilty of both slovenliness of language, and the resultant foolishness. MERS took well defined words, words that had been in use for hundreds of years, and mangled them. They didn't tell the rest of us that they were changing these words; they probably didn't realize it themselves. They took words like "mortgagee", which dates back to the 1500s, and blurred its meaning. As a result, thousands of cases were needlessly litigated nationwide. If MERS had simply explained itself clearly, or used the new terms developed in "MERS, Notes and Mortgages", the nation would have been spared much drama. This is demonstrated in Chapters 8, 10, and 11 of the Tutorial, and in the Chapter: "Clean Up MERS", which show that hundreds, if not thousands, of cases litigated around the subject of MERS were completely unnecessary. It wasted untold millions, and distracted the nation from the real issues causing the mortgage meltdown.

3. Lack of Accountability due to Poor Execution

Another two words that were mangled by MERS are "vice-president", and "secretary". And this brings us to the third reason for our national confusion**. 3. There is so much confusion about MERS because of the lack of transparency due to poor execution.** Back in the day, when I was growing up, an organization had one vice president. Then to placate all the talented candidates for president of the organization, one became five or ten. MERS took this to a new level. They have tens of thousands of vice presidents. Of course, not one of them is really a vice president of MERS – or even an employee of MERS. They are simply employees of lending institutions, or law firms, or title processors, who are authorized to sign for MERS. The President of MERS testified in Congress that he didn't know how many such certified officers were registered with MERS. Beyond the general confusion caused to the nation, title examiners are exasperated because we have no idea who executes the millions of assignments and satisfactions that are executed in the name of MERS. We discuss this in Chapter 16 of the Tutorial and in the Chapter: "Clean up MERS".

4. Misuse of Legal Fictions

One final answer. **4. There is so much confusion about MERS because of the misuse of legal fictions.** For some reason, which I still haven't figured out, MERS decided that it would be efficient for their members to bring foreclosure actions in the name of MERS instead of the lender's own name. This is a legal fiction that confused everyone. Even worse, MERS created a fiction within this fiction. When necessary, MERS allowed the lender to claim that MERS was the Holder of the note. (All this is explained below.) But this was a fiction too far. Leonardo DiCaprio found this out in the movie "Inception": when you create a fiction within a fiction, you can lose your bearings. MERS created an "Inception" of fictions which no one knew how to untangle. Fortunately, despite winning its case in court, MERS stopped this practice. After July 22, 2011, members of MERS may not initiate foreclosure in the name of MERS, and consequently, there never is a need for MERS to purport to be the Holder of the note.

In the chapter "Could MERS Ever Really Be the Holder of the Note" we will discuss this legal fiction.

MERS was created to execute a good idea that solved a pressing economic problem. And despite multiple warnings in the press and in law reviews about MERS' coming demise, MERS is here to stay because at the core, MERS does fulfill a useful economic function. But due to poor use of words, the misuse of legal fictions, lack of transparency through poor execution, and the mixing of law and title, MERS unnecessarily made a continent-wide mess.

These are the four underlying themes for the confusion about MERS.

II. CLEAN UP MERS: AN OPERATIONAL ANALYSIS OF MERS – SIX PROBLEMS

1. Poorly Drafted Instruments.

MERS operates on the Honor System. It is headquartered in Reston, Virginia. That's the seat of a mortgage registry (with around 70 million mortgages) together with its legal, corporate and business departments. But the thousands of members of MERS, who are spread across the country, are responsible for drafting mortgages, deeds of trust, assignments and satisfactions. In addition, tens of thousands of certified officers execute those assignments and satisfactions. The problem is that these instruments are drafted and executed without supervision by MERS. Because of the rampant confusion across the country as to MERS' real interest in property, many thousands of instruments are incorrect, confusing, nonsensical and damaging.

1) **Poorly Drafted Mortgages**: In the course of my work I have seen many MERS mortgages which are suspect. For instance, a mortgage (Document 1) recorded in Miami-Dade County (O.R. Book 25622, Page 4928) states, in paragraph (D), that MERS is the Lender (of $460,000.00!) That cannot be true. MERS does not lend money. Is this a valid mortgage? Did this mortgage really pledge property against a loan that was made to the borrower by an unidentified party?

After Recording Return To:
Hadlock Title Services, Inc.
679 Worcester Road
Natick, MA 01760

MIN: 100029500016653598

———————————— [Space Above This Line for Recording Data] ————————————

MORTGAGE

DEFINITIONS

Words used in multiple sections of this document are defined below and other words are defined in Sections 3, 11, 13, 18, 20 and 21. Certain rules regarding the usage of words used in this document are also provided in Section 16.

(A) "Security Instrument" means this document, which is dated March 22, 2007, together with all Riders to this document.

(B) "Borrower" is ▇▇▇▇▇▇▇▇▇▇▇▇▇▇▇▇▇▇▇▇▇▇▇. Borrower is the mortgagor under this Security Instrument.

(C) "MERS" is Mortgage Electronic Registration Systems, Inc. MERS is a separate corporation that is acting solely as a nominee for Lender and Lender's successors and assigns. MERS is the mortgagee under this Security Instrument. MERS is organized and existing under the laws of Delaware, and has an address and telephone number of P.O. Box 2026, Flint, MI 48501-2026, tel. (888) 679-MERS.

(D) "Lender" is MERS. Lender is a Corporation organized and existing under the laws of the State of Florida. Lender's address is 4901 SW 80 Street, Miami, FL 33143. Lender is the mortgagee under this Security Instrument.

(E) "Note" means the promissory note signed by Borrower and dated March 22, 2007. The Note states that Borrower owes Lender Four Hundred Sixty Thousand Dollars (U.S. $460,000.00) plus interest. Borrower has promised to pay this debt in regular Periodic Payments and to pay the debt in full not later than April 1, 2037.

(F) "Property" means the property that is described below under the heading "Transfer of Rights in the Property."

(G) "Loan" means the debt evidenced by the Note, plus interest, any prepayment charges and late charges due under the Note, and all sums due under this Security Instrument, plus interest.

(H) "Riders" means all Riders to this Security Instrument that are executed by Borrower. The following Riders are to be executed by Borrower [check box as applicable]:

☐ Adjustable Rate Rider   ☐ Condominium Rider   ☐ Second Home Rider
☐ Balloon Rider   ☐ Biweekly Payment Rider X 1-4 Family Rider
☐ Planned Unit Development Rider   X Other (specify) Exhibit A

FLORIDA–Single Family–Fannie Mae/Freddie Mac UNIFORM INSTRUMENT   Form 3010 1/01 (page 1 of 16 pages)

AS
M

DOCUMENT #1

14

Document 2 is an example of an absurdly drafted mortgage recorded in Osceola County (O. R. Book 3034, Page 1993). At the end of the second line of paragraph (c) the following appears: "MERS is the beneficiary under this Security Instrument". This instrument was executed and recorded in Florida which is a Lien-Theory State. (For an explanation of this term and the other terms used on this page, please see the Tutorial.) In a Lien-Theory State, MERS, together with the lender, is the "mortgagee", not the "beneficiary" of the security instrument. There are multiple problems with this instrument: Did this instrument actually create a security interest to guarantee the underlying debt? Who then is the mortgagee? Is this instrument valid?

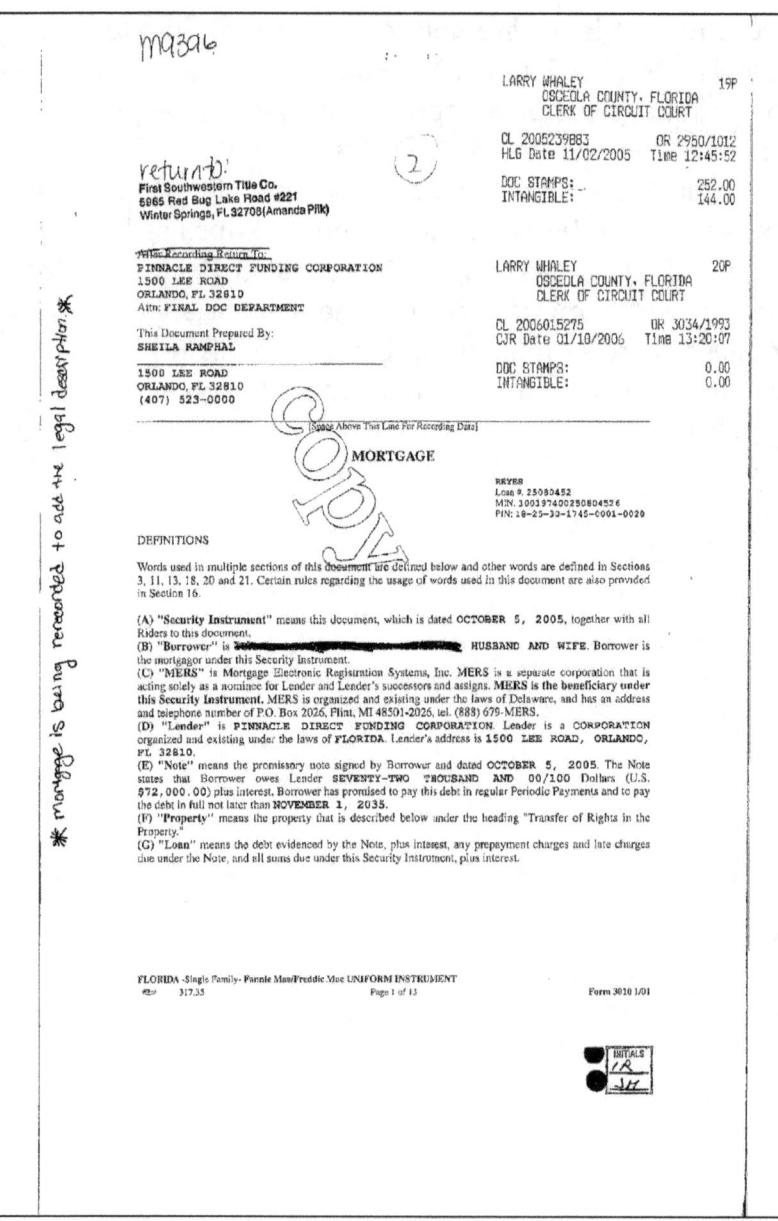

m93a6

return to:
First Southwestern Title Co.
5965 Red Bug Lake Road #221
Winter Springs, FL 32708(Amanda Pilk)

After Recording Return To:
PINNACLE DIRECT FUNDING CORPORATION
1500 LEE ROAD
ORLANDO, FL 32810
Attn: FINAL DOC DEPARTMENT

This Document Prepared By:
SHEILA RAMPHAL

1500 LEE ROAD
ORLANDO, FL 32810
(407) 523-0000

[Space Above This Line For Recording Data]

MORTGAGE

REYES
Loan #. 25080452
MIN:30019740025080452 6
PIN: 18-25-30-1745-0001-0020

DEFINITIONS

Words used in multiple sections of this document are defined below and other words are defined in Sections 3, 11, 13, 18, 20 and 21. Certain rules regarding the usage of words used in this document are also provided in Section 16.

(A) "Security Instrument" means this document, which is dated OCTOBER 5, 2005, together with all Riders to this document.
(B) "Borrower" is ███████████████████████████ HUSBAND AND WIFE. Borrower is the mortgagor under this Security Instrument.
(C) "MERS" is Mortgage Electronic Registration Systems, Inc. MERS is a separate corporation that is acting solely as a nominee for Lender and Lender's successors and assigns. MERS is the beneficiary under this Security Instrument. MERS is organized and existing under the laws of Delaware, and has an address and telephone number of P.O. Box 2026, Flint, MI 48501-2026, tel. (888) 679-MERS.
(D) "Lender" is PINNACLE DIRECT FUNDING CORPORATION. Lender is a CORPORATION organized and existing under the laws of FLORIDA. Lender's address is 1500 LEE ROAD, ORLANDO, FL 32810.
(E) "Note" means the promissory note signed by Borrower and dated OCTOBER 5, 2005. The Note states that Borrower owes Lender SEVENTY-TWO THOUSAND AND 00/100 Dollars (U.S. $72,000.00) plus interest. Borrower has promised to pay this debt in regular Periodic Payments and to pay the debt in full not later than NOVEMBER 1, 2035.
(F) "Property" means the property that is described below under the heading "Transfer of Rights in the Property."
(G) "Loan" means the debt evidenced by the Note, plus interest, any prepayment charges and late charges due under the Note, and all sums due under this Security Instrument, plus interest.

FLORIDA -Single Family- Fannie Mae/Freddie Mac UNIFORM INSTRUMENT
            317.35   Page 1 of 13   Form 3010 1/01

INITIALS

* mortgage is being recorded to add the legal description *

DOCUMENT #2

16

2) Poorly Drafted Assignments. There are thousands, possibly millions, of assignments in the public records of the 50 states which declare that besides assigning the mortgage, MERS is also assigning the note. Document 3 is a typical, assignment, recorded in O.R. Book 48141, Page 328, Broward County. The offensive paragraph reads as follows:

".….does hereby grant, sell, assign, transfer and convey......all **beneficial** interest under that certain Mortgage described below **together with the notes(s)** and obligations therein described and the money due and to become due thereon with interest......."

There are two different mistakes here:

a) MERS neither owns, holds, nor possesses the note. Furthermore, MERS has no authority to assign the note. A MERS assignment of mortgage is not generated until after the note has been sold, endorsed and delivered. At that point, a paralegal at some law firm, or title clearing firm, is ordered to draft an assignment of mortgage to complete and perfect the transfer the note. The assignment of mortgage is drafted **after** the note has already been negotiated and transferred. As such, the assignment of mortgage only perfects and memorializes that transfer; it does not actually do anything to the note. This purported assignment of the note caused the whole *Bellistri* fiasco.

b) Secondly, MERS needs to transfer actual title to the mortgage, not just the "beneficial interest". Yet nowhere in the assignment is there a transfer of title to the mortgage.

At best, these badly drafted assignments cause confusion. At worst, they cause economic damage. There are thousands of such poorly drafted assignments in Florida alone. Nationwide, there might be hundreds of thousands, or even millions of poorly drafted assignments. As such, some, if not all MERS' assignments are defective.

Recording Requested By:
Bank of America
Prepared By: Mercedes Judilla
888-603-9011
When recorded mail to:
CoreLogic
450 E. Boundary St.
Attn: Release Dept.
Chapin, SC 29036

DocID# 83712856646873398
Property Address:
1245 SW 46th Ave Unit 1210
Pompano Beach, FL 33069-6435
FL0-AJ4 14998201   8/11/2011

③

This space for Recorder's use

MIN #: 1002480-0000203019-5   MERS Phone #: 888-679-6377

ASSIGNMENT OF MORTGAGE

For Value Received, the undersigned holder of a Mortgage (herein "Assignor") whose address is 3300 S.W. 34TH AVENUE, SUITE 101 OCALA, FL 34474 does hereby grant, sell, assign, transfer and convey unto THE BANK OF NEW YORK MELLON FKA THE BANK OF NEW YORK, AS TRUSTEE FOR THE CERTIFICATEHOLDERS OF CWHEQ, INC., HOME EQUITY LOAN ASSET BACKED CERTIFICATES, SERIES 2006-S4 whose address is 101 BARCLAY ST - 4W, NEW YORK ,NY 10286 all beneficial interest under that certain Mortgage described below together with the note(s) and obligations therein described and the money due and to become due thereon with interest and all rights accrued or to accrue under said Mortgage.

Original Lender: GMFS, LLC.
Original Borrower(s):   ███████████, SINGLE WOMAN
Date of Mortgage: 5/25/2006
Original Loan Amount: $29,798.00
Recorded in Broward County, FL on: 6/1/2006, book OR42129, page 1330 and instrument number 106124945

IN WITNESS WHEREOF, the undersigned has caused this Assignment of Mortgage to be executed on
08/24/2011
MORTGAGE ELECTRONIC REGISTRATION SYSTEMS, INC.

By: _____   By: _____
Dominique Johnson   Cynthia Santos
Assistant Secretary   Assistant Secretary

_____   _____
Witness: Beverly Brooks   Witness: Malik Basurto

State of California
County of Ventura

On Aug 24th 2011 before me, Deborah L Beard, Notary Public, personally appeared Dominique Johnson and Cynthia Santos, who proved to me on the basis of satisfactory evidence to be the person(s) whose name(s) is/are subscribed to the within instrument and acknowledged to me that he/she/they executed the same in his/her/their authorized capacity(ies), and that by his/her/their signature(s) on the instrument the person(s) or the entity upon behalf of which the person(s) acted, executed the instrument.

I certify under PENALTY OF PERJURY under the laws of the State of California that the foregoing paragraph is true and correct.

WITNESS my hand and official seal.

Notary Public: Deborah L Beard   (Seal)
My Commission Expires: June 26, 2013

DEBORAH L. BEARD
Commission # 1853913
Notary Public - California
Ventura County
My Comm. Expires Jun 26, 2013

DOCUMENT #3

18

3) Poorly Drafted Satisfactions and Releases. Below I discuss whether MERS should ever execute a satisfaction of mortgage. Here, I would just like to point out that if MERS is going to execute a satisfaction, at a minimum it should be drafted correctly. In Document 4 (Satisfaction recorded in O.R. Book 49275, Page 355) MERS is declared to be "…owner and holder of a certain Mortgage…". Neither term is correct. At best, MERS can be said to the holder of title to the mortgage. But it is not the "owner" of the mortgage. Neither is MERS the "holder" of a mortgage, since there is no such thing as "holder" of a mortgage. "Holder" of the note is a construct in law. There is no "holder" of the mortgage.

Loan #: 89958825

Document Prepared By:
E.Lance/NTC, 2100 Alt. 19
North, Palm Harbor, FL 34683
(800)346-9152

When Recorded Return To:
GREEN TREE SERVICING LLC
C/O NTC 2100 Alt. 19 North
Palm Harbor, FL 34683

SATISFACTION OF MORTGAGE

KNOW ALL MEN BY THESE PRESENTS: That MORTGAGE ELECTRONIC REGISTRATION SYSTEMS, INC. ('MERS') AS NOMINEE FOR GMFS LLC, is the owner and holder of a certain Mortgage Deed executed by ~~████████████~~ recorded in Official Records Book 42129, Page 1330 or Document # 105124945, in the office of the Clerk of the Circuit Court of BROWARD County, Florida, upon the property situated in said State and County as more fully described in said Mortgage.
Hereby acknowledges full payment and satisfaction of said note and Mortgage Deed, and surrender the same as canceled, and hereby directs the Clerk of the said Circuit Court to cancel the same of record.

IN WITNESS WHEREOF, the signature of said owner and holder by its ASST. SECRETARY this 26th day of November in the year 2012.
MORTGAGE ELECTRONIC REGISTRATION SYSTEMS, INC. ('MERS') AS NOMINEE FOR GMFS LLC, ITS SUCCESSORS AND ASSIGNS

By: _____
DANIEL THOMPSON
ASST. SECRETARY

All Authorized Signatories whose signatures appear above are employed by NTC and have reviewed this document and supporting documentation prior to electronically affixing their electronic signature.

_____   _____
WENDY RAMIREZ   WITNESS   FRANCE MOSS   WITNESS

STATE OF FLORIDA
COUNTY OF PINELLAS
The foregoing instrument was acknowledged before me on this 26th day of November in the year 2012, by Daniel Thompson as ASST. SECRETARY for MORTGAGE ELECTRONIC REGISTRATION SYSTEMS, INC. ('MERS') AS NOMINEE FOR GMFS LLC, ITS SUCCESSORS AND ASSIGNS, who, as such ASST. SECRETARY being authorized to do so, executed the foregoing instrument for the purposes therein contained.
He/she/they is (are) personally known to me.

_____
ELIZABETH A. MUSTARD - NOTARY PUBLIC
COMM EXPIRES: 08/27/2015

Elizabeth A. Mustard
Notary Public State of Florida
My Commission # EE 088429
Expires August 27, 2015
Bonded Thru Notary Public Underwriters

GTSRC 17873606 1002480000020130195 MERS PHONE 1-888-679-MERS DOCR T261211-4408 ERCNFL1

17873606

DOCUMENT #4

Another defective instrument is Document 5 (O.R. Book 48047, Page 686). This Release of Mortgage states that MERS "…has received full payment and satisfaction…". This of course is impossible since MERS is not in the loop when it comes to money. The final owner or group of investors received the funds, not MERS.

To clean up this mess, MERS should proofread and approve all documents that are executed in the name of MERS, by generating general templates and policing what is signed in its name.

ORIGINAL DOCUMENT

Recording Requested by
TROY L. JOHNSON
SUNTRUST MORTGAGE, INC.
1001 SEMMES AVENUE
RVW 3013
RICHMOND, VA 23224

When Recorded Mail To:
SUNTRUST MORTGAGE, INC.
SHERRI FARMER
PAYOFF DEPT RVW 3013
P. O. BOX 27406
RICHMOND, VA 23286-9437

Release of Mortgage

Loan Number: 0145121812
MERS ID: 100010401451216127
VRU Number: 1-888-679-6377
KNOW ALL MEN BY THESE PRESENTS that MORTGAGE ELECTRONIC REGISTRATION SYSTEMS, INC. holder of a certain
Mortgage, whose parties, dates and recording information are listed below, does hereby acknowledge that it has received full payment
and satisfaction of the same, and in consideration thereof, does hereby cancel and discharge said Mortgage.
Original Mortgagor: ▬▬▬▬▬▬▬▬▬▬
Original Mortgagee: MERS, AS NOMINEE FOR ADVANCE CAPITAL SERVICES, INC.
Dated: 06/20/2006 Recorded: 07/06/2008 in Book/Reel/Liber: 42350 Page/Folio: 1086-1108 as Instrument Number: 106228349 In the
Official Records in the County of Broward State of FL affecting Real Property and more particularly, described on said Mortgage
referred to herein.
Tax ID Number:
Property Address: 9000 NW 28TH DR #1-103, CORAL SPRINGS, FL 33065
Legal:
IN WITNESS WHEREOF, MORTGAGE ELECTRONIC REGISTRATION SYSTEMS, INC. by the officers duly authorized, has duly
executed the foregoing instrument.
Today's Date: 07/18/2011
MORTGAGE ELECTRONIC REGISTRATION SYSTEMS, INC.
By:

Gabrielle Beck

GABRIELLE BECK, Vice-President

Notary Acknowledgement:
This instrument was acknowledged before me, STARR LACKS , a notary public in and for Richmond (City) county in the state of VA on
07/18/2011 by GABRIELLE BECK , as Vice-President of MORTGAGE ELECTRONIC REGISTRATION SYSTEMS, INC.
Witness my hand and official seal,

Starr Lacks

STARR LACKS Notary Public for Richmond (City) County, VA
My Commission Expires: 10/31/2011
7151846

STARR LACKS
Notary Public
Commonwealth of Virginia
7151846
My Commission Expires Oct 31, 2011

Prepared By: GABRIELLE BECK

DOCUMENT #5

2. How can the Courts understand MERS when MERS' agents don't understand MERS?

Here is an example of the mischief that is caused by a poorly drafted assignment.

The Missouri Court of Appeals, in *Ocwen v. Bellistri* ruled that Ocwen, the Holder of the note, had no standing to pursue its foreclosure. The fatal flaw, according to the Court, was an assignment that purported to transfer the note (!) from MERS to Ocwen. The court recited the relevant language (which is identical to the mangled Florida assignment quoted above):

"... together with any and all notes and obligations therein described or referred to, the debt respectively secured thereby and all sums of money due and to become due." (page 6).

Since the note was not transferred from MERS, the court ruled that Ocwen did not own the note and had no standing. The judge obviously did not understand that MERS never transfers the note since MERS never has the note. MERS is simply the mortgagee-in-title. Therefore, from the fact that MERS did not transfer the note - it cannot be inferred that Ocwen is not the owner of the note. Ocwen simply bought the note from the previous owner. The note was correctly transferred to Ocwen without the good offices of MERS.

The attorney for MERS missed the boat twice in this case. First, he/she did not explain the mechanics of MERS to the court in an appropriate fashion. Secondly, all the attorney had to do was to show that Ocwen was the current owner of the note; not because MERS transferred the note to Ocwen, but because the original lender transferred the note to Ocwen.

Each time a court refuses to allow MERS to be a plaintiff in a foreclosure action, the media, the blogs, and law commentators seize on the case as further proof of the lack of standing of MERS. But there are many different reasons for such a decision. When the court says that MERS cannot start a foreclosure action because the lender for which it acts does not Hold the note (which is a factual determination), that is very different than stating that MERS never has standing as a plaintiff in a foreclosure action (which is a legal determination). In the former case, the court is not telling us anything that we did not know for the last 400 years. That is very different than declaring point blank that legally, MERS cannot be a plaintiff in a foreclosure action. This confusion occurs because MERS is not properly policing its members.

In this fiasco, like in the movie "Inception", we have four layers of absurdity nestled one inside the other. First, an authorized agent for MERS drafts, executes and records an absurd instrument. Secondly, the judge of a state appeals court uses that defective instrument to draw an incorrect conclusion. Third, the attorney for MERS fails to set the record straight. Fourth, the media misinterprets the meaning of the case, drawing incorrect national conclusions from the flaw of the specific situation. Finally, various law professors mangle their analysis of MERS by failing to take into account a title analysis of the case. And those professors are cited by the New York Times.

To clean up this mess, MERS must do much more to define its terms clearly, explain itself to its own workers and "certified" officers, and to the public at large.

3. The Chain of Title of the Security Interest is Often Mangled

1) The Transfer of Notes is Not Always Reported to MERS

According to the agreement between MERS and its members, a transfer of the note between one member and another must be reported to MERS immediately. But this rule has not always been obeyed. In many cases in different states, the courts have asked MERS to prove that the lender - in whose name a foreclosure action has been started - actually has the note. On many occasions, the note had already moved on to another institution, or has not yet been endorsed and delivered to the plaintiff. This sloppiness is inexcusable. MERS should have enforced reporting, certainly when it was to have been the plaintiff in a foreclosure act.

2) Sometimes, MERS executes Satisfactions when it is no longer in Title.

Look again at Document 3 in which MERS assigns the note to The Bank of New York Mellon (O.R. Book 48141, Page 328). Now look at Document 4 (recorded three months later in O.R. Book 49275, Page 355, Broward County) in which MERS purports to satisfy that same note. How can MERS record a satisfaction when MERS is no longer on title and no longer has any authority to do so? How can title examiners rely on this satisfaction when MERS had no authority to execute it?

Here is another example. Document 6 is an Assignment of Mortgage from MERS to U.S. Bank (O.R. Book 46552, Page 997). Then next instrument in the chain is Document 7 (O.R. Book 47937, Page 319) in which MERS purports to record a Satisfaction of Mortgage. If MERS already assigned this mortgage to U.S. Bank, on what authority does it execute a satisfaction?

ASSIGNMENT OF MORTGAGE

SPACE FOR RECORDING ONLY 3.5 (MS H-

FOR VALUE RECEIVED, on or before July 10, 2009, the undersigned, MORTGAGE ELECTRONIC
REGISTRATION   SYSTEMS,   INCORPORATED,   ("Assignor")   whose   address   is
_____ assigned,
transferred and conveyed to: U.S. BANK NATIONAL ASSOCIATION, AS TRUSTEE OF THE
HOMEBANC MORTGAGE TRUST 2007-1 MORTGAGE PASS-THROUGH CERTIFICATES,
("Assignee")   whose   address   is

its successors and/or assigns, all of the right, title, and interest of Assignor in and to that certain Mortgage (the
"Mortgage") dated December 20, 2006 and recorded January 02, 2007 in Official Records Book 43355 at Page
918 of the public records of BROWARD County, Florida, encumbering the following-described real property:

> LOT 30, OF CARLTON ESTATES 2, ACCORDING TO THE PLAT THEREOF, AS
> RECORDED IN PLAT BOOK 153, AT PAGE 4, OF THE PUBLIC RECORDS OF
> BROWARD COUNTY, FLORIDA

as the same may have been amended from time to time; together with the Note and indebtedness secured thereby.

MORTGAGOR(S): ████████████

IN WITNESS WHEREOF, Assignor has executed and delivered this Instrument on
Sept ___, 2009.

MIN # 100022100229450424

Witness
Typed Name: Yer Yang

Witness
Typed Name: Christina Reagan

MORTGAGE ELECTRONIC REGISTRATION
SYSTEMS, INCORPORATED
By: _____
Typed Name: Liquenda Allotey
Title: VP

Attest: _____
Typed Name: Greg Allen
Title: VP   (Affix Corporate Seal)

STATE OF   Minnesota
COUNTY OF   Dakota

BEFORE ME, the undersigned, personally appeared   Liquenda Allotey
and   Greg Allen   as   VP   and   VP
respectively, and known to me to be the persons that executed the foregoing Instrument, and acknowledged that
they executed the foregoing as its duly authorized officers and that such execution was done as the free act and deed
of MORTGAGE ELECTRONIC REGISTRATION SYSTEMS, INCORPORATED, this 2 day of Sep
, 2009.

Notary Public: James A. Chua

JAMES A. CHUA
NOTARY PUBLIC - MINNESOTA
MY COMMISSION
EXPIRES JAN 31, 2013

My commission expires:

Recording requested by, prepared by and return to:
Deborah Pullen
Florida Default Law Group, P.L.
P.O. Box 25018
Tampa, Florida 33622-5018
F09075192-JPMORGAN CHASE BANK, N.A.

FILE_NUMBER: F09075192

DOC_ID: M001100

F09075192   *M001100*

DOCUMENT #6

FLORIDA SATISFACTION

Prepared by/Record and Return To:
RALPH A BUCCI
1560 SW 99TH TER.

DAVIE   , FL. 13324-6419
Loan Number: 0022943042
Min: 100022100229450434
MERS Phone, if applicable 1-888-679-6377
Outbound Date: 04/27/11

SATISFACTION OF MORTGAGE

KNOW ALL MEN BY THESE PRESENTS: MORTGAGE ELECTRONIC REGISTRATION SYSTEMS, INC.,
the Owner and Holder of a certain Mortgage Deed executed by ▓▓▓▓▓▓▓▓▓▓▓▓▓▓▓▓▓
HOMEBANC MORTGAGE CORPORATION bearing the date of December 20, 2006, recorded January 2, 2007 in
Official Records Volume/Book 43355 Page 918 Document 106709796 in the Office of the Clerk of the Circuit
Court of BROWARD County, State of Florida, securing a certain note in the principal sum of $728,000.00 and
certain promises and obligations set forth in said Mortgage Deed, upon the property situated in said State and
County described as follows, to wit:

Property Address: 3440 CARLTON LANE, DAVIE, FL 33330

Hereby acknowledges full payment and satisfaction of said Note and Mortgage Deed, and surrenders the same as
cancelled, and hereby directs the Clerk of said Circuit Court to cancel the same of record.

In witness whereof MORTGAGE ELECTRONIC REGISTRATION SYSTEMS, INC. has caused these
presents to be executed in its name, and its corporate seal to be hereunto affixed, by its proper officers
thereto duly authorized, May 9, 2011.

MORTGAGE ELECTRONIC REGISTRATION SYSTEMS, INC.

INGRID WHITTY
Vice President

Signed, sealed and delivered
in the presence of:

ARCOLA FREEMAN

Vicki Strickland

State of Louisiana
Parish/County of: OUACHITA

On this May 9, 2011, before me a Notary Public, the undersigned officer, personally appeared INGRID
WHITTY, known to me (or satisfactorily proven) to be the person whose name is subscribed to the within
instrument and did depose and say that he/she executed the same for the entity named and for the purposes therein
contained.
IN WITNESS WHEREOF, I set my hand and signature which certifies as my seal.

PAMELA WILCHER - 80556
Notary Public
LIFETIME

FL.10
09/10/07

DOCUMENT #7

3) Sometimes, There Are Multiple Assignments out of MERS for the Same Note

Title examiners often find that more than one assignment of mortgage has been executed by MERS for the same note. As explained above, these assignments are drafted and executed at thousands of locations around the country, without any actual supervision by MERS. The result is that the chain of title for the security interest is often mangled and unclear. Here's an example from the Public Records of Broward County. Document 8 is an assignment recorded in O.R. Book 48942, Page 1587. MERS assigns a mortgage to Federal National Mortgage Association. On the next page, (O.R. Book 48942, Page 1588) the very same mortgage is assigned by CitiMortgage to Federal National Mortgage Association (Document 9). How is that possible?

FLORIDA
COUNTY OF BROWARD
POOL NO.
LOAN NO. (18856939) [LB0392]

Assignment-Interv.-Executed
WHEN RECORDED MAIL TO:
SETERUS, INC
14523 SW MILLIKAN WAY, #200
BEAVERTON, OR 97005
ATTN

(8)

ASSIGNMENT OF MORTGAGE
KNOW ALL MEN BY THESE PRESENTS, that
MORTGAGE ELECTRONIC REGISTRATION SYSTEMS, INC.
SOLELY AS NOMINEE FOR FLAGSTAR BANK, FSB ITS SUCCESSORS AND ASSIGNS,

located at 1901 E VOORHEES ST, SUITE C, , DANVILLE, IL 61834
"Assignor," in consideration of the sum of TEN DOLLARS ($10.00) and other good
and valuable consideration paid by FEDERAL NATIONAL MORTGAGE ASSOCIATION

located at 14221 DALLAS PARKWAY, SUITE 1000 DALLAS, TX 75254
"Assignee", does hereby grant, bargain, assign, transfer and set over unto Assignee
a certain indenture of mortgage bearing the date of JUNE 29, 2005
made by ████████████ SINGLE MAN, AS HIS SOLE & SEPARATE PROPERTY
and recorded in
Book 40097 , page 1699 , Clerk's File #105192794 public records
of BROWARD County, Florida, upon the following described property:

AS DESCRIBED ON SAID MORTGAGE REFERRED TO HEREIN.

TOGETHER WITH all rights accrued or to accrue under said Mortgage.
TO HAVE AND TO HOLD the same unto the said Assignee, its successors and assigns forever.
IN WITNESS WHEREOF these presents has caused these presents to be executed in its
name by its proper officers thereunto duly authorized this 1st day of
NOVEMBER 2011 .

Mortgage Electronic Registration Systems, Inc.

BY: _____
REBECCA HIGLEY
ASSISTANT SECRETARY

STATE OF IDAHO)
) ss
COUNTY OF BONNEVILLE)

On NOVEMBER 1, 2011 , before me, the undersigned, personally appeared
REBECCA HIGLEY who is known to me to be the person who executed
the within instrument as the ASSISTANT SECRETARY
of the Corporation that executed the within
instrument and acknowledged to me that the Corporation executed the within instrument pursuant to its by-laws or a resolution of its board of directors.

WITNESS my hand and official seal.

_____
VICKIE SORG (COMMISSION EXP. 08-18-17)
NOTARY PUBLIC

VICKIE SORG
NOTARY PUBLIC
STATE OF IDAHO

PREPARED BY
_____
KARLEEN MAUGHAN
240 TECHNOLOGY DRIVE
IDAHO FALLS, ID 83401

P=S.002.00640.338
C=s.658.0714

MIN 100052550069343183 MERS PHONE: 1-888-679-6377
J-LH8040110AI.s.31153

DOCUMENT #8

N

⑨

INSTRUMENT PREPARED BY AND
WHEN RECORDED MAIL TO:
Seterus, Inc.
14523 SW Millikan Way, Suite 200
Beaverton, OR 97005

18856939-770774338
INV 1698975064
MIN #: 100052550089343183
APN / Tax ID: 51-41-12-10-0320

This area for recording office use

Corporate Assignment of Mortgage

--- Contact Federal National Mortgage Association for this instrument c/o Seterus, Inc., 14523 SW Millikan Way #209, Beaverton, OR 97005, telephone # 1-866-570-5277, which is responsible for receiving payments.

FOR VALUE RECEIVED, **CitiMortgage, Inc.**, with and address of **1000 Technology Drive, O'Fallon, MO 63368**, hereby grants, assigns and transfers to

Federal National Mortgage Association, a United States Corporation

with an address of in care of LBPS, Inc., 14523 SW Millikan Way, #200, Beaverton, OR 97005

All beneficial interest under that certain Mortgage dated 06/29/2005 and executed by ████████████

The beneficiary being **FLAGSTAR BANK, FSB**

Recorded on 07/19/2005 in book 40097 at page 1699 as Instrument No. 105192794 of Official Records in the County Recorder's office of **BROWARD**, State of Florida.

Lot 23 Block 1 of HOLLYWOOD COUNTRY ESTATES according to the Plat thereof, as recorded in Plat Book 24 Page 9 of the Public Records of Broward County, Florida.

Property Address: 1528 N 58TH AVE, HOLLYWOOD, FL 320214543

(Corporate Seal)

CitiMortgage, Inc. By Seterus, Inc., fka IBM Lender Business Process Services, Inc., its Attorney in Fact

Name: Justin M. Burns
Title: Loan Administration Assistant Vice President

Witness: Adrienne Paddock

Witness: Melinda Carrey

STATE OF OR
COUNTY OF Washington

On 9/23/2011 before me, Andrew M Shapley, Notary Public, Personally appeared Justin M. Burns, who is the Loan Administration Assistant Vice President of Seterus, Inc., Personally known to me or proved to me on the basis of satisfactory evidence to be the person(s) whose name(s) is/are subscribed to the within instrument and acknowledged to me that he/she/they executed the same in his/her/their authorized capacity(ies), and that by his/her/their signature(s) on the instrument the person(s), or the entity upon behalf of which the person(s) acted, executed the instrument.
WITNESS my hand and official seal.

OFFICIAL SEAL
ANDREW MARK SHAPLEY
NOTARY PUBLIC - OREGON
COMMISSION NO. 457041
MY COMMISSION EXPIRES MARCH 28, 2015

Andrew M Shapley, Notary Public

DOCUMENT #9

4) Sometimes, the Mortgage is Assigned to a Non-Member, before the Note

Another mess-up occurs when a mortgage is assigned by MERS to a non-member who proceeds to initiate foreclosure, before the note itself is transferred.

To clean up this mess, MERS should demand real-time reporting of note transfer, with penalties for non-compliance.

4. Robo-Signing by "vice-presidents" of MERS

In 2010 the U.S. took notice that affidavits were being signed by lending institutions, and by their attorneys, in a haphazard fashion. It was reported in the press that some institutions were signing many thousands of affidavits at a time, and they were then being notarized by the thousand, without any acknowledgment by the signor. This is a violation of notary requirements and constituted fraud upon the court. Once this practice became public knowledge, many banks "froze" all of their foreclosure activity until the problem could be sorted and fixed.

As stated above, MERS appointed many thousands of people to be "certified vice-presidents" and "certified assistant secretaries", and authorized them to sign in the name of MERS. Some of them engaged in such robo-signing. For instance, many assignments by Cheryl Samons of the Law Office of David J. Stern are clearly invalid. (According to newspaper reports, the firm actually closed because of alleged fraudulent practices originating with Ms. Samons). I have seen assignments with her signature on the signature line and the identical signature on the notary signature line. Either she was notarizing herself, or the notary was forging her signature. I have also shown some of her MERS assignments to ex-workers from that law office and they told me that the signatures were fraudulent. Take a look at Documents 10, 11, and 12 which are MERS assignments recorded in O.R. Book 45554, Page 854, O.R. Book 45768, Page 1599 and O.R. Book 45892, Page 219.

Prepared by: DAVID J. STERN, ESQ
Record Return to: 900 South Pine Island Road Suite 400
Plantation, FL 33324-3920
08-50470 (HFRM)

This space is for recording purposes only

ASSIGNMENT OF MORTGAGE

KNOW ALL MEN BY THESE PRESENTS:

THAT MORTGAGE ELECTRONIC REGISTRATION SYSTEMS, INC.

Residing or located at C/O HOMECOMINGS FINANCIAL, LLC, ONE MERIDIAN CROSSING, STE 100, MINNEAPOLIS, MN 55423, herein designated as the assignor, for and in consideration of the sum of $1.00 Dollar and other good and valuable consideration, the receipt of which is hereby acknowledged, does hereby grant, bargain, sell, assign, transfer and set over unto U.S. BANK NATIONAL ASSOCIATION, AS TRUSTEE residing or located at C/O HOMECOMINGS FINANCIAL, LLC, ONE MERIDIAN CROSSING, STE 100, MINNEAPOLIS, MN 55423 herein designated as the assignee, the mortgage executed by ███████████████████████, A SINGLE MAN recorded in BROWARD County, Florida in book 43451 and page 54 encumbering the property more particularly described as follows:

UNIT 24-03 OF QUATRAINE AT JACARANDA GARDENS, CONDOMINIUM ONE, ACCORDING TO THE DECLARATION THEREOF, RECORDED IN OFFICIAL RECORDS BOOK 13349, PAGE 95, AMENDED BY INSTRUMENTS RECORDED IN OFFICIAL RECORDS BOOK 13335, PAGE 809, OFFICIAL RECORDS BOOK 13596, PAGE 994, OFFICIAL RECORDS BOOK 13785, PAGE 859, OFFICIAL RECORDS BOOK 14010, PAGE 334, CLERKS FILE NO. 87-080455, OFFICIAL RECORDS BOOK 14583, PAGE 544, & CLERKS FILE NO. 87-345974, OF THE PUBLIC RECORDS OF BROWARD COUNTY, FLORIDA, SAID LANDS SITUATE, LYING AND BEING IN BROWARD COUNTY, FLORIDA.

together with the note and each and every other obligation described in said mortgage and the money due and to become due thereon

TO HAVE AND TO HOLD the same unto the said assignee, its successors and assigns forever, but without recourse on the undersigned.

Pursuant to the provisions of Sec. 689.071, Florida Statutes, the within named Trustee has the power and authority to protect, conserve and to sell, or to lease, or to encumber, or otherwise to manage and dispose of the above-described mortgage and the real property encumbered thereby.

In Witness Whereof, the said Assignor has hereunto set his hand and seal or caused these presents to be signed by its proper corporate officers and its corporate seal to be hereto affixed, this 17 day of July, 2008 but effective as of the 27th day of March, 2008.

Signed in the presence of: MORTGAGE ELECTRONIC REGISTRATION SYSTEMS, INC

ATTEST: BY:
PRINT NAME: CHERYL SAMONS
TITLE: ASSISTANT SECRETARY

WITNESS:
Print Name: _____

WITNESS: Michelle E. Camacho
Print Name:

STATE OF FL
COUNTY OF Broward

PERSONALLY APPEARED BEFORE ME, the undersigned authority in and for the aforesaid county and state, on this the 17 day of July, 2008 within my jurisdiction, the within named CHERYL SAMONS who is personally known to me and who acknowledged to me that (s)he is ASSISTANT SECRETARY and that for and on behalf of MORTGAGE ELECTRONIC REGISTRATION SYSTEMS, INC., and in its full and deed (s)he executed the above and foregoing instrument, after first having been duly authorized by MORTGAGE ELECTRONIC REGISTRATION SYSTEMS, INC to do so.

WITNESS my hand and official seal in the County and State last aforesaid this 17 day of July, 2008

NOTARY PUBLIC   Michelle E. Camacho

MICHELLE L. CAMACHO
MY COMMISSION # DD682913
EXPIRES: March 24, 2012

DOCUMENT #10

Prepared by
Record & Return to: DAVID J. STERN, ESQ
900 South Pine Island Road Suite 400
Plantation, FL 33324-3920
(file number)

ASSIGNMENT OF MORTGAGE

KNOW ALL MEN BY THESE PRESENTS:

THAT MORTGAGE ELECTRONIC REGISTRATION SYSTEMS, INC.

Residing or located at c/o CITIMORTGAGE, INC., C/O CITIMORTGAGE, INC., P.O. BOX 790014, ST. LOUIS, MO 63179, herein designated as the assignor, for and in consideration of the sum of $1.00 Dollar and other good and valuable consideration, the receipt of which is hereby acknowledged, does hereby grant, bargain, sell, assign, transfer and set over unto CITIMORTGAGE, INC., residing or located at: C/O CITIMORTGAGE, INC., P.O. BOX 790014, ST. LOUIS, MO 63179 herein designated as the assignee, the mortgage executed by ███████████████ recorded in BROWARD County, Florida at book 43393 and page 825 encumbering the property more particularly described as follows:

LOT 9, IN BLOCK 37, OF LAKE FOREST SECTION FOUR, ACCORDING TO THE PLAT THEREOF, AS RECORDED IN PLAT BOOK 38, AT PAGE 4, OF THE PUBLIC RECORDS OF BROWARD COUNTY, FLORIDA.

together with the note and each and every other obligation described in said mortgage and the money due and to become due thereon

TO HAVE AND TO HOLD the same unto the said assignee, its successors and assigns forever, but without recourse on the undersigned.

In Witness Whereof, the said Assignor has hereunto set his hand and seal or caused these presents to be signed by its proper corporate officers and its corporate seal to be hereto affixed, this ___ day of _October_ 2008 but effective as of the 26th day of November, 2007.

Signed in the presence of: MORTGAGE ELECTRONIC REGISTRATION SYSTEMS, INC

ATTEST: BY:
                                                            PRINT NAME: CHERYL SAMONS
WITNESS   TITLE: ASSISTANT SECRETARY

WITNESS
Print Name: _Helene Cerois-Hall_

STATE OF FLORIDA
COUNTY OF BROWARD

PERSONALLY APPEARED BEFORE ME, the undersigned authority in and for the aforesaid county and state, on this this ___ day of _October_, 2008 within my jurisdiction, the within named _Cheryl Samons_ who is personally known to me and who acknowledged to me that (s)he is ASSISTANT SECRETARY and that for and on behalf of MORTGAGE ELECTRONIC REGISTRATION SYSTEMS, INC. and as its act and deed (s)he executed the above and foregoing instrument, after first having been duly authorized by MORTGAGE ELECTRONIC REGISTRATION SYSTEMS, INC. to do so.

WITNESS my hand and official seal in the County and State last aforesaid this ___ day of _October_, 2008.

                                                            NOTARY PUBLIC

DOCUMENT #11

Prepared by
Record address to: DAVID J. STERN, ESQ.
                      900 South West Street Road Suite 100
                      Plantation, FL 32324-0509
                      (954) NOT. ASGT 1

This space is for recording purposes only

ASSIGNMENT OF MORTGAGE

KNOW ALL MEN BY THESE PRESENTS:

THAT MORTGAGE ELECTRONIC REGISTRATION SYSTEMS, INC.

Residing or located at c/o WELLS FARGO BANK, N.A. 3476 STATEVIEW BLVD., FT. MILL, SC 29715 herein designated as
the assignor, for and in consideration of the sum of $1.00 Dollar and other good and valuable consideration, the receipt of which is
hereby acknowledged, does hereby grant, bargain, sell, assign, transfer and set over unto US BANK NATIONAL ASSOCIATION,
AS TRUSTEE FOR STRUCTURED ASSET SECURITIES CORPORATION TRUST 2007-EQ1 residing or located at: C/O
AMERICA'S SERVICING COMPANY, 3476 STATEVIEW BLVD, FT. MILLS, SC 29715 herein designated as the assignee, the
mortgage executed by ███████████████████████ corded in BROWARD County, Florida at book 43292 and
page 281 encumbering the property more particularly described as follows:

UNIT 2-102, TUSCANY NO. 3, A CONDOMINIUM, ACCORDING TO THE DECLARATION OF CONDOMINIUM
THEREOF, AS RECORDED IN OFFICIAL RECORDS BOOK 41149, AT PAGE 937, OF THE PUBLIC RECORDS OF
BROWARD COUNTY, FLORIDA, TOGETHER WITH THE UNDIVIDED INTEREST IN THE LIMITED COMMON
ELEMENTS AND/OR COMMON ELEMENTS APPURTENANT TO SUCH UNIT.

together with the note and each and every other obligation described in said mortgage and the money due and to become due thereon

TO HAVE AND TO HOLD the same unto the said assignee, its successors and assigns forever, but without recourse on the
undersigned

Pursuant to the provisions of Sec. 689.071, Florida Statutes, the within named Trustee has the power and authority to protect,
conserve and to sell, or to lease, or to encumber, or otherwise to manage and dispose of the above-described mortgage and the real
property encumbered thereby.

In Witness Whereof, the said Assignor has hereunto set his hand and seal or caused these presents to be signed by its proper corporate
officers and its corporate seal to be hereto affixed, this 22 day of December , 20 08 but effective as of the 4 day of October,
2007.

Signed in the presence of: MORTGAGE ELECTRONIC REGISTRATION SYSTEMS, INC.

ATTEST: BY:
WITNESS: PRINT NAME: CHERYL SAMONS
Print Name: _____   TITLE: ASSISTANT SECRETARY
WITNESS:
Print Name: _____

STATE OF Florida
COUNTY OF Broward

    PERSONALLY APPEARED BEFORE ME, the undersigned authority in and for the aforesaid county and state, on this
the 22 day of December , 2008 , within my jurisdiction, the within named CHERYL SAMONS who is personally known
to me and who acknowledged to me that (s)he is ASSISTANT SECRETARY and that for and on behalf of MORTGAGE
ELECTRONIC REGISTRATION SYSTEMS, INC. and as its act and deed (s)he executed the above and foregoing instrument, after
first having been duly authorized by MORTGAGE ELECTRONIC REGISTRATION SYSTEMS, INC. to do so.

WITNESS my hand and official seal in the County and State last aforesaid this 22 day of December 20 08

                                                   NOTARY PUBLIC

Notary Public, State of Florida
Esteban Romero
My Commission DD730849
Expires 11/00/2011

DOCUMENT #12

One would have hoped that the 2010 scandal would have ended the practice. But I have found that the practice continues. On June 28, 2011 there are twelve assignments recorded in St. Johns County, O.R. Book 3449, Pages 653, 724, 730, 733, 890, 914, 928, 932, 972, 974, 976, and 1032. All are signed by "Derrick White Vice President", and witnessed by Ashley Braband and Debra Goyer. Two of them are shown here in Documents 13 and 14. In all twelve assignments the signatures are identical, and in the identical position on the instrument. One possibility is that these documents were photocopied and therefore constitute fraud. Another possibility is that all four signatures were signed electronically. But even then we have a different problem. Derrick White signed as Vice President of MERS as nominee for Principal Residential Mortgage, Inc., and assigned the mortgage to Citimortgage. But look at Document 15 which shows Derrick White, still in Pinellas County, signing as Vice President of Citimortgage.

When Recorded Return To:
CitiMortgage, Inc.
C/O NTC 2100 Alt. 19 North
Palm Harbor, FL 34683

CMI Loan #: 0012304109
Investor #: 372518281

ASSIGNMENT OF MORTGAGE

FOR GOOD AND VALUABLE CONSIDERATION, the sufficiency of which is hereby acknowledged, the undersigned, MORTGAGE ELECTRONIC REGISTRATION SYSTEMS, INC. AS NOMINEE FOR QUICKEN LOANS INC, ITS SUCCESSORS AND ASSIGNS, (ASSIGNOR), (MERS Address: P.O. Box 2026, Flint, Michigan 48501-2026) by these presents does convey, grant, sell, assign, transfer and set over the described mortgage together with the certain note(s) described therein together with all interest secured thereby, all liens, and any rights due or to become due thereon to **CITIMORTGAGE, INC., WHOSE ADDRESS IS 1000 TECHNOLOGY DRIVE, O'FALLON, MO 63368 (636)261-2484, ITS SUCCESSORS OR ASSIGNS, (ASSIGNEE).**

Said Mortgage was made by ~~████████████~~ AND ~~████████████~~ AND ~~████████████~~ and was recorded in Official Records of the Clerk of the Circuit Court of ST JOHNS County, Florida, on Book 2689, Page 699, or Instrument #

upon the property situated in said State and County as more fully described in said mortgage.

Date: 06/21/2011
MORTGAGE ELECTRONIC REGISTRATION SYSTEMS, INC. AS NOMINEE FOR QUICKEN LOANS INC, ITS SUCCESSORS AND ASSIGNS

_____
DERRICK WHITE   VICE PRESIDENT

_____   _____
ASHLEY BRABAND   WITNESS   DEBRA OGYER   WITNESS

Document Prepared By: E. Lance/NTC, 2100 Alt. 19 North, Palm Harbor, FL 34683 (800)346-9152
CGMAS 14333295 MIN 100039046777302189 MERS PHONE 1-888-679-MERS EFRMFL1

14333295

DOCUMENT #13

37

STATE OF FLORIDA
COUNTY OF PINELLAS

The foregoing instrument was acknowledged before me this 21st day of June in the year 2011, by DERRICK
WHITE as VICE PRESIDENT for MORTGAGE ELECTRONIC REGISTRATION SYSTEMS, INC. AS
NOMINEE FOR QUICKEN LOANS INC., ITS SUCCESSORS AND ASSIGNS, who, as such VICE PRESIDENT
being authorized so to do, executed the foregoing instrument for the purposes therein contained. He/she/they is (are)
personally known to me.

MIRANDA AVILA, NOTARY PUBLIC
Comm. Expires: 08/22/2014

Notary Public State of Florida
Miranda Avila
My Commission EE019063
Expires 08/22/2014

Document Prepared By: E. Lance/NTC. 2100 Alt. 19 North, Palm Harbor, FL 34683 (800)346-9152
CGMAS 14333295 MIN 100039040677302189 MERS PHONE 1-888-679-MERS ELGRMFL 1

14333295

DOCUMENT #13 – Page 2

38

When Recorded Return To:
CitiMortgage, Inc.
C/O NTC 2100 Alt. 19 North
Palm Harbor, FL 34683

CMI Loan #: 0006259660
Investor #: 722003227

ASSIGNMENT OF MORTGAGE

FOR GOOD AND VALUABLE CONSIDERATION, the sufficiency of which is hereby acknowledged, the undersigned, MORTGAGE ELECTRONIC REGISTRATION SYSTEMS, INC. AS NOMINEE FOR PRINCIPAL RESIDENTIAL MORTGAGE INC, ITS SUCCESSORS AND ASSIGNS, (ASSIGNOR), (MERS Address: P.O. Box 2026, Flint, Michigan 48501-2026) by these presents does convey, grant, sell, assign, transfer and set over the described mortgage together with the certain note(s) described therein together with all interest secured thereby, all liens, and any rights due or to become due thereon to CITIMORTGAGE, INC., WHOSE ADDRESS IS 1000 TECHNOLOGY DRIVE, O'FALLON, MO 63368 (636)261-2484, ITS SUCCESSORS OR ASSIGNS, (ASSIGNEE).

Said Mortgage was made by ▓▓▓▓▓▓▓▓▓▓ AND ▓▓▓▓▓▓▓▓▓▓ and was recorded in Official Records of the Clerk of the Circuit Court of ST. JOHNS County, Florida, in Book 1965, Page 1723, or Instrument #

upon the property situated in said State and County as more fully described in said mortgage.

Date: 06/21/2011
MORTGAGE ELECTRONIC REGISTRATION SYSTEMS, INC. AS NOMINEE FOR PRINCIPAL RESIDENTIAL MORTGAGE INC, ITS SUCCESSORS AND ASSIGNS

_____
DERRICK WHITE   VICE PRESIDENT

_____   _____
ASHLEY BRABAND   WITNESS   DEBRA GOYER   WITNESS

Document Prepared By: E. Lance/NTC, 2100 Alt. 19 North, Palm Harbor, FL 34683 (800)346-9152
CGMAS 14340355 MIN 10002660006259660I MERS PHONE 1-888-679-MERS BFRMFLI

14340355

DOCUMENT #14

STATE OF FLORIDA
COUNTY OF PINELLAS

The foregoing instrument was acknowledged before me this 21st day of June in the year 2011, by DERRICK WHITE, as VICE PRESIDENT for MORTGAGE ELECTRONIC REGISTRATION SYSTEMS, INC. AS NOMINEE FOR PRINCIPAL RESIDENTIAL MORTGAGE INC, ITS SUCCESSORS AND ASSIGNS, who, as such VICE PRESIDENT being authorized so to do, executed the foregoing instrument for the purposes therein contained. He/she/they is (are) personally known to me.

MIRANDA AVILA, NOTARY PUBLIC
Comm. Expires: 08/22/2014

Notary Public State of Florida
Miranda Avila
My Commission EE019063
Expires 08/22/2014

Document Prepared By: E. Lance/NTC, 2100 Alt. 19 North, Palm Harbor, FL 34683 (800)346-9152
CGMAS 14340355 MIN 100026600062596601 MERS PHONE 1-888-679-MERS EFRMFL1

14340355

DOCUMENT #14 – Page 2

40

When Recorded
Return To:
CitiMortgage, Inc.
C/O NTC 2100 Alt. 19 North
Palm Harbor, FL 34683

Prepared By:
E.Lance/NTC, 2100 Alt. 19 North,
Palm Harbor, FL 34683
(800)346-9152

MidFirst L#: 0054785531
Citi L#: 0647230818

ASSIGNMENT OF
MORTGAGE / DEED OF TRUST

FOR GOOD AND VALUABLE CONSIDERATION, the sufficiency of which is hereby acknowledged, the undersigned, Citimortgage, Inc. successor in interest by merger to ABN AMRO Mortgage Group, Inc. a/k/a ABN AMRO MORTGAGE INC, WHOSE ADDRESS IS 1000 TECHNOLOGY DRIVE, O'FALLON, MO, 63368, (ASSIGNOR), by these presents does convey, grant, sell, assign, transfer and set over the described MORTGAGE/DEED OF TRUST with all interest secured thereby, all liens, and any rights due or to become due thereon to MIDFIRST BANK, A FEDERALLY CHARTERED SAVINGS ASSOCIATION, WHOSE ADDRESS IS 999 N.W. GRAND BOULEVARD SUITE 100, OKLAHOMA CITY, OK 73118 (800)654-4566, ITS SUCCESSORS OR ASSIGNS, (ASSIGNEE),

Said MORTGAGE/DEED OF TRUST is dated 03/17/2005, by:  AND WIFE, ████████, AS TENANTS BY THE ENTIRETY WITH RIGHTS OF SURVIVORSHIP to ABN AMRO MORTGAGE GROUP, INC. and recorded in Book 2,191 at page 763 Doc# of the Records of Deeds in the office of the Chancery Clerk of DESOTO County, Mississippi.

Dated on 12/ 02 /2011 (MM/DD/YYYY)
Citimortgage, Inc. successor in interest by merger to ABN AMRO Mortgage Group, Inc. a/k/a ABN AMRO
MORTGAGE INC

By: _____
DERRICK WHITE   VICE PRESIDENT

STATE OF FLORIDA   COUNTY OF PINELLAS
The foregoing instrument was acknowledged before me on 12/ 02 /2011 (MM/DD/YYYY), by DERRICK WHITE as VICE PRESIDENT for Citimortgage, Inc. successor in interest by merger to ABN AMRO Mortgage Group, Inc. a/k/a ABN AMRO MORTGAGE INC, who, as such VICE PRESIDENT being authorized to do so, executed the foregoing instrument for the purposes therein contained. He/she/they is (are) personally known to me.

_____
KARIN ENRIQUE CHANDIAS
Notary Public - State of FLORIDA
Commission expires: 05/22/2015

> Karin Enrique Chandias
> Notary Public State of Florida
> My Commission # EE 095894
> Expires May 22, 2015

CMMFA 14904679 -- 12.01.2011 CJ3400034 FORM5\FRMMS1

14904679

DOCUMENT #15

Clearly, MERS has no control over what is being done in its name. **To clear up this mess, MERS must police what is being done in its name.**

5. MERS and the UCC have to Rethink Assignments of Mortgages

Before MERS, the assignment of mortgage also served as an assignment of the debt (i.e. the note). As the scholar Tiffany explained:

Tiffany, The Law of Real Property and Other Interests in Land, VOL. 3 – 1920 – p. 2528-29:

"The question is properly one of the construction of the language used, and in arriving at the proper construction, evidence of the sense in which that language is ordinarily used is of primary importance. The expression "assignment of mortgage" is almost universally used, not only by the general public, but also by the Legislature, the courts, and the legal profession, to describe the transfer of the totality of the mortgagee's rights, that is, his right to the debt as well as to the lien securing it; and to hold, as these cases apparently do, that when one in terms assigns a mortgage, he intends, not an effective transfer of his rights as creditor against the land, but a transfer of his lien alone, which is an absolute nullity, not only ignores this ordinary use of the term "mortgage", but is also in direct contravention of the well-recognized rule that an instrument shall if possible be construed so as to give it a legal operation."

But this is no longer the case because:

1) Due to the nature of the MERS system, the assignment of mortgage is executed, and subsequently recorded, after the

note has already been negotiated. Sometimes months or years later. The assignment is just a notice to the public of the transaction and not the transaction itself.

2) MERS does not have the power to assign the note, regardless of the countless assignments that state otherwise.

To compound the problem, should the assignment of mortgage remain silent about the note, according to Restatement (Third) of Property (Mortgages) 5.4(b) the note will pass to the assignee of the mortgage or the deed-of-trust as the case may be. But so many assignments have been recorded out of order that such a presumption would cause havoc.

The UCC has solved one aspect of the problem as follows. As noted previously, the doctrine since 1872 is that the mortgage follows the note. But what happens when the note is lost? The relatively new Section 9 states that the assignment of mortgage proves ownership – unless there is an indication to the contrary. In other words, if all we have is the assignment of mortgage, then that proves ownership (by which Tiffany's doctrine survives). But if another party can show payment, and/or possession of an endorsed note, then the assignment of mortgage plays second fiddle. Actual possession or proof of payment trumps the recorded assignment.

I phrase this new reality as follows:

The mortgage follows the note - in Equity.
The note follows the mortgage - in Title - as long as there is no indication to the contrary.

This reformulates the Supreme Court's doctrine in order to reflect the current economic reality. What does this mean? On one hand, the beneficial owner of the debt (the note) must simultaneously be the beneficiary of the pledge of the property (the mortgage). The note and mortgage are an organic whole and cannot be separated. The owner of one is always the owner of both. But in terms of the public record - i.e. in terms of tracing ownership of that note and mortgage - the chain of title is reflected in the chain of title holders of the mortgage; since it is the mortgage and its assignments that are recorded in the public record. The very term "chain of **title**" gives witness to the fact that the public record is concerned with ownership-in-**title.**

To sum up this section, MERS and the UCC have to work out new frameworks for assignment so that:

1)   MERS is not seen as assigning the note;

2)   Silence in the assignment of mortgage as to the note does not constitute an assignment of the note;

3)   The assignment clarifies that it is being recorded as public information and is not an assignment of debt.

4)   There is transparency as to who signed the assignment. This is similar to the demands of the next section.

6. Should MERS execute Satisfactions of Mortgages?

One final problem. I find many satisfactions of mortgages in the public record executed by MERS. This makes no sense theoretically or practically.

In terms of theory, since MERS does not hold the note, or receive money, or keep track of money, what is the logic in having MERS execute the satisfaction? MERS simply holds title to the security interest, the mortgage. As such it could execute a Release of Mortgage, upon instruction of the lender. But it should not execute satisfactions.

Practically speaking, instruments in which MERS purports to satisfy the mortgage are not really executed by an employee of MERS. Such an instrument is executed by a so-called "vice-president" or "secretary" of MERS who is really an employee of the note holder or their agent. Title examiners are expected to accept these satisfactions on a daily basis even though it is clear that they are one more fiction propagated by the sloppy execution of the MERS business model. The court recognizes this problem. For instance, in the Nevada case **In re Mitchell,** (p. 11) the judge wrote:

"There appears to be absolutely no requirement that these Certifying officers have any knowledge of the loan in question."

And on page 13: "..yet there is no evidence that these Certifying Officers have adequate personal knowledge of the facts."

To clean up this mess, I propose the following:

1) Satisfactions should not be executed in the name of MERS. When the time comes for a mortgage to be satisfied, MERS should assign the mortgage to the final Holder of the note. That party should execute the satisfaction. That way, the chain of mortgage ends with the final Holder of the note, as it should. This would be the ideal solution.

2) In the alternative, when the "vice-president" or "secretary" of MERS executes a satisfaction:

a) that person should declare for whom he/she works. That would allow the title examiner to determine if indeed the signor did indeed have knowledge of the financial transaction by which the note has been paid off.

b) MERS should have a publicly viewable website listing all of its "vice-presidents" and "secretaries". If MERS can maintain a database of 70 million mortgages, it can also maintain a database of its 30,000 officers. That way, a title examiner could check to see whether a satisfaction was indeed signed by a certified officer of MERS, and receive confirmation as to the employer of the person signing the satisfaction.

In sum: We saw in the accompanying Tutorial that the legal model of MERS does work once the terms are clearly defined and used correctly. But here we see that there is much to be desired in the way that MERS executes that model. MERS has come up short in:

1) **Draftsmanship** – of mortgages, assignments and satisfactions. The current situation, in which title examiners daily examine MERS documents which are badly drafted, misconceived, or even fraudulent is unacceptable.

2) **Education** – of its workers, certified officers, and the public at large.

3) **Policing** the performance of its members, in both the reporting of note transfer and in robo-signing. The lack of supervision by MERS of what is going on among its thousands of members causes real damage to the economy.

4) **Transparency.** MERS should maintain a publicly viewable database of its pool of "certified officers."

5) **Satisfactions**. MERS should either stop the execution of satisfactions in its name or provide some mechanism to eliminate the ambiguities we now face.

By ramping up the standards of draftsmanship, education, and policing of its members, MERS can eliminate the lack of transparency and accountability that pervades its operation, and finally succeed in acting as an agent of efficiency in modernizing America's real estate markets.

III. ABOLISH THE BEARER NOTE – AND MAYBE THE PHYSICAL NOTE ALSO.

The bearer note stands at the intersection of two shifting paradigms. On one hand, paper as a store of value is being phased out of the marketplace. On the other hand, analog record keeping is giving way to digital data storage. Because of these two shifting paradigms, I propose that the note should no longer be a bearer instrument (though it must continue to be negotiable). And while we're at it, we should abolish the physical note altogether.

How, when and why did paper come to be used as a store of value? Interestingly, paper as a store of value began only a few years after paper was introduced into Europe. And how did paper arrive in Europe to begin with?

Paper was invented by the Chinese. The first known specimens date back to the second century B.C., though paper production might have begun earlier. While the Egyptians started to make writing material from the papyrus plant a thousand years earlier, and while the word "paper" evolved from the word "papyrus", paper cannot be made from papyrus. Papyrus was made by cutting strips of pulp from the papyrus plant and laying them side by side in two layers. The bottom layer was laid horizontally; the top layer vertically. The mass was moistened, pressed and dried; then hammered and polished. In contrast, paper is made from a cellulose based plant which is beaten down, or chemically processed, so that each fiber floats separately. The mass is then suspended on webbing, drained, dried and beaten. The mechanics might be similar, but the results are very different.

It took close to a thousand years for paper production to arrive in the Middle East from China. In the early 700's the Chinese Tang Empire began a rapid expansion westward conquering parts of Central Asia and threatening the new Muslim caliphates of the Mideast. In 751, the armies of the Abbasid Caliphate, which had recently seized power in the Fertile Crescent, met the Chinese army in the valley of the Talas River, now situated on the border of between Kazakhstan and Kyrgyzstan. The Abbasid armies routed the Chinese. That battle cemented the ascent of the Abbasids in the Middle East, and was also the beginning of the end of the Tang dynasty. The Chinese empire never expanded beyond that point. But their technology did, since the Abbasids realized that several of their Chinese prisoners knew the art of papermaking. This might be legend though sources actually identify one of the artisans by the name of Tou Houan. (Allegedly, he returned to China years later and wrote an account of how he taught the Arabs various crafts such as china pottery and papermaking.) Maybe traders brought the technology westward independently of this battle. Or maybe the paper makers of Central Asia suddenly found the door open to the Middle East. In any case, the now-forgotten Battle of Talas is considered the catalyst for bringing paper-making from China to the Middle East, and within 10 years, Baghdad was a major paper producer.

Over the next four centuries, paper making technology made its way west as Moslem rule spread across the Mid-East and North Africa and into Southern Europe. Paper bundles were called "rismah" in Arabic. That word evolved in to the English "ream" for 500 sheets. Paper was used not only for making books, but for wrapping and other purposes. By the year 1000 paper was being made in Sicily, and by 1150, in Southern Spain, both under Muslim rule. At that time, the Normans conquered Sicily, establishing a Kingdom there in 1132. They adopted the customs and technology of their Islamic subjects including paper making. Since Normans were Christian, they served as the bridge for bringing papermaking into the Christian world, through the Italian Peninsula directly to their north. By 1220 Italians were producing paper. A year later, the Holy Roman Emperor Frederick II declared that official documents written on paper were invalid. The Pope issued a similar decree. But this did not prevent the spread of paper production all over Italy. By the late 1200's, the Fabriano paper mill was established in Ancona. They are still producing paper to this day.

But how did paper become a store of monetary value? When Marco Polo arrived in China, the Chinese had already been printing paper money for 200 years. He reported this novel idea to Europe when he returned in 1295 and recorded his travels. In Book 2, Chapter 24, Marco Polo explains that the inner bark of the Mulberry Tree is converted into paper which is cut into various sizes and imprinted with the seals and names of various officials. Since it was a capital crime (punishable by beheading) to refuse to accept paper money, Chinese citizens had no choice but to accept it as legal tender. This was a shocking idea then (even today there are outliers who decry the Federal Reserve) and it did not catch on in Europe for another three centuries. But the ability of paper to act as a store of value had already begun in Italy, and its explosive development had nothing to do with Marco Polo.

The main impetus for treating paper as a store of value came from the renewal of trade between Europe and the Middle East in the wake of the Crusades. From the fall of the Roman Empire in the fifth century until 1096, when the first Crusade was called, trade had ceased between these two neighboring geographic areas. The lack of a central authority to maintain roads, the lack of metal currency in which to do trade, and the impoverished state of war-torn, agricultural Europe, all acted as impediments to trade. But the tens of thousands of Western European soldiers who journeyed to rich Constantinople in the Crusades, and then onto Palestine, were exposed not only to goods that had not been seen in Europe in centuries (e.g. spices and silk) but also to entirely new products such as paper and books. As the soldiers returned home from their respective Crusades (spread out over two centuries) demand for these goods spurred a renewal of trade. And the renewal of trade created demand for credit, liquidity, and monetary transferability. This in turn spurred the creation of new financial institutions and instruments needed to finance that trade.

Starting in 1100 Italian financiers adapted, invented, and engineered the methods, financial instruments and banking institutions that underlie modern commerce. To become mathematically efficient, they stopped using Roman numeral and learned to work with Arabic numerals, the "zero", and later on, the decimal point. They invented double entry bookkeeping. And they developed international banking by establishing branches in every port of Europe.

The first banks were foreign-exchange traders and money lenders who, starting in the 1100's were assigned a bench, or "banc" in the public squares of Florence, Venice and Genoa, to transact exchange of foreign currencies and to accept deposits. (If the bank lost the deposits –as when King Edward of England refused to repay his loans - the bench was broken or "rotta" in Italian; namely the bank was "banc-rotta", root of our term - bankrupt. They expanded to all corners of Christian Europe setting up branches from London, Paris, and Bruges in the West to Constantinople in the East. And they developed the financial instruments needed for foreign exchange, credit, liquidity and transferability

Most important for this discussion, they developed a new financial instrument – **the bill of exchange**. In contrast to a promissory note, which is a contract between two parties, the bill of exchange is a contract between 3 or more parties. The following description is light on the mechanics of the transaction; my sole purpose is to describe the matrix of players.

a) It started simple – with three players – executing a transfer of funds. A merchant named Spicehandler sells his mid-eastern wares in Florence for 1000 Florins, but does not want to transport the gold back to Constantinople to buy new goods. So he deposits the gold with a Florentine banker on Sept. 1 who gives him a bill of exchange, which instructs a correspondent bank in Constantinople to give Spicehandler Venetian Ducats on Oct. 1 when he arrives. (Of course, the exchange rate includes a commission for the bank's work). How does the bank in Florence pay the bank in Constantinople? It doesn't. The Florentine bank pays out Florins in Florence upon instruction of the bank in Constantinople. The two banks honor each other's instructions, which are simply pieces of paper called bills of exchange, and settle the differences periodically. It is important to remember that the bank's agent paid out in a different currency (Venetian ducats) than the bank had originally collected.

b) Lets add a fourth party. Spicehandler sells his mid-eastern wares in Florence for a thousand Florins, but does not travel back to Constantinople to buy new goods. He deposits the gold with a Florentine banker on Sept. 1 who gives him a bill of exchange, which instructs the Constantinople branch of the bank to give Spicehandler's agent Venetian Ducats on Oct. 1. Spicehandler sends the bills to his agent who goes to the bank on Oct. 1 to collect the money. We now have four parties transacting a transfer of funds.

c) Now let's add credit. Spicehandler needs money to buy Italian leather to ship to Constantinople. This time, the bank gives Spicehandler a loan of 970 Florins. He, in exchange, signs a "draft" which simply instructs his agent in Constantinople to pay 1000 Florins to the bank's agent on Jan. 1 (after the leather is sold). The bank sends the "draft" to its agent in Constantinople. The agent gets the drafts on Oct. 1 and goes to Spicehandler's agent to see if he will honor it. Spicehandler's agent acknowledges that he will honor the draft in 90 days by signing the drafts; this is called "acceptance" since he accepts the obligation to pay by adding his signature to the draft. On Jan. 1, the bank's agent comes to collect, and Spicehandler's agent pays Venetian Ducats to the bank's agent, as agreed. Today, one example of this occurs when you buy travelers cheques, which is really a bill of exchange. The four parties are the two banks, the traveler, and the overseas merchant. You buy dollar denoted travelers cheques from a U.S. bank. These cheques simply instruct an overseas bank to pay out the noted amounts to any merchant presenting them. When you buy souvenirs from a Parisian storekeeper, and pay with a dollar-denoted traveler cheque, she goes to her bank who buys them from her for Euros. The two banks settle between themselves.

d) Finally, bills of exchange can be created by two merchants. A leather merchant (not the bank) extends Spicehandler 970 Florins worth of credit. In exchange, Spicehandler signs the draft. The merchant sends the drafts to Constantinople where the leather merchant's agent presents the draft to Spicehandler's agent for collection. On a personal level, I saw my father, in New York, sell merchandise to manufacturers from Venezuela. I saw them sign drafts in New York for payment in 90, 120, and 150 days. I went with my father to give the drafts to the bank which acted as a collecting agent. The drafts were sent to Caracas where the buyer's bank accepted the drafts by signing them. When the time came, the banks in Venezuela collected the money and remitted them to our bank in New York. Nothing had changed in the mechanics of the transaction in 800 years.

The earliest surviving **bill of exchange** was drafted in 1156. Two brothers borrowed money in Genoa in one currency and agreed to repay the bank's agents in Constantinople in another currency. This solved both their credit needs, and the need to exchange currencies. (The following year, 1157, the first national bank ever created in Europe was formed in Venice. It lasted until 1797.) The bill of exchange was revolutionary in that solved various problems simultaneously. 1) The bill of exchange allowed for the safe transfer of funds through bookkeeping instead of the physical transport of bullion. 2) It created the paradigm for government currency, as we shall see. 3) Finally, it allowed Italian Christians to engage in lending by skirting the prohibition against usury. The key here is the fact that the transaction is closed out in a different currency than the original transaction. Whether the Bill of Exchange was created as a funds transfer (examples 1 and 2 above) or as a transaction financed with credit (examples 3 and 4 above) the final financial transfer must take place in a different currency than the original loan or deposit. At some point, these Italian bankers had a Eureka moment in which they realized that they could hide the interest charge inside the foreign exchange transaction. Since foreign exchange fluctuated just as wildly in those years as they do today, who was to say that the exchange rate was exorbitant? And since the funds were returned to the lender through a reverse bill of exchange, the two transactions together created a smokescreen as to the underlying interest earned in the transaction. Since Church theologians defined interest as the receipt of more currency than originally borrowed, Bills of Exchange fell outside the realm of the prohibited transaction. What was received was a different currency.

So far, we have a lot of paper with instructions floating around, but we don't yet have paper as a store of value. To do this, we have to add one more element - **transferability by assignment** of ownership of the bill of exchange. Here's the scenario. Spicehandler deposits 1000 Florins in Florence and in return is given a bill of exchange which instructs a Constantinople bank to pay him Venetian Ducats in 90 days. Spicehandler travels back to Constantinople and has the Bill stamped "accepted". Then he travels to Venice and sees a shipment of goods being offered at a very low rate. But how will he pay? All he has is a piece of paper with instructions to a Bank located in Turkey! Well here is where the Italians showed true genius. Spicehandler goes into a bank in Venice, not necessarily a branch of the Florentine bank where he deposited his money. He sells his bill of exchange to that bank by signing the back of the bill (now known as "endorsing" the instrument). Of course the bank takes its fee. Now, instead of the original four parties to the contractual arrangement, we have a fifth party. What does the Venetian bank do with the draft it bought? It can settle with the Florentine bank; or collect from the agent in Constantinople. Or sell it to a different party.

Suddenly, a piece of paper worth a fraction of a cent, with a set of instructions on it, is valued at 1000 florins! That piece of paper now has become a store of value. As long as a financial transaction is limited to the original parties to the transaction, there is no creation of a store of value. The paper that memorializes the transaction is just a piece of paper. But when a party (a person or entity) which was not one of the parties to the original transaction, agrees to buy the a piece of paper which spells out a financial obligation, that new party is declaring that the piece of paper has value – even immense value. **Paper as a store of value involves a piece of paper containing a written financial obligation that is acquired by a party not involved in the original commercial transaction.**

Before continuing, let us pay homage: The Italians accomplished all of this within a very short period of time. They resolved the great, and growing need for credit and liquidity by mastering the newly imported technology of paper production, learning the newly imported Arabic numeral system, inventing double entry bookkeeping, developing the bill of exchange, and establishing the mechanism by which those bills of exchange could be marketable. Bills of exchange have been the backbone of international trade for centuries and became known as "the pillar of commerce". (In fact, during the 18th and early 19th century, bills of exchange made up more of the money supply of England than did printed money.)

But why did the bill of exchange quickly become so freely marketable, while the other types of debt did not? For the previous thousand years, Jewish law did not recognize the marketability of personal debt. And it would take centuries for other types of debt to catch up to bills of exchange both in commerce and in law. What does the bill of exchange have that allowed it to become the equivalent of money while real estate debt or credit card debt could not do so until recently? After all, they all embody a financial obligation. Furthermore, the mechanics of endorsement are the same for all types of debt. Debt can be endorsed either 1) to a specific person or 2) "en blanc", meaning "in blank" (i.e. whoever holds or "bears" the paper, can claim ownership). So why did the debt embodied by a bill of exchange become freely transferrable, and a source of liquidity, centuries before other types of debt became marketable? Any paper that memorializes a financial obligation should be marketable!

The answer is that there is a difference in who owes the money. In a promissory note (an obligation between two parties) the borrower is an individual. His creditworthiness is an unknown. It might be bad or worthless. In a bill of exchange, the debtor is the bank!

How so? In a bill of exchange, there actually are two different trans-actions; the first is a commercial exchange and the second is a financial exchange. In the first, there is either a purchase of goods on credit between two merchants, or a loan taken by a borrower from a lender, or the deposit of funds with a banking institution. The buyer/borrower is called the "drawer" because he draws up, and signs, the drafts. The drafts instruct a "drawee", which is a bank, or merchant house to pay out the money to a party designated by the lender or seller. That designated party, called the "payee" (because the money is eventually paid to this party) is sent the drafts. The payee presents the drafts to the drawee (the bank or merchant bank who will pay). Once the drawee signs the drafts – an act called "acceptance" – **the bills of exchange becomes a financial obligation of the drawee**. At that point, the bill of exchange is no longer the obligation of the original borrower/buyer. Nor is it a bank guarantee of the obligation of the original borrower/buyer. The bill of exchange is an obligation of the accepting bank or merchant house itself!

Why would anyone buy those bills? Because of the identity of the drawee. Why wouldn't any Italian feel safe with a bill that states he is owed 1000 florins by the Bank of Medici or another well-known Italian bank? Why wouldn't an Englishman accept a bill in which The Bank of Rothschild promises to pay 1000 sterling to the holder? Why wouldn't an American accept a bill in which Chase Manhattan promises to pay $1,000.00? After all, the original merchant seller/lender agreed to lend the money because he knew that the drawee was large and honorable. In effect, once the drawee accepts the draft by signing it, paper money has been created. The financial obligation of the drawee is a saleable item! While the bill of exchange started to be transferable because of the trust in the drawee, its widespread use was a function of the enforceability of the obligation of the drawee. At first, the drawee's obligation was enforceable because it was the "custom of the merchants". Eventually, enforceability became the law of the land.

Professor James Steven Rogers points out that by the early 1600s, the idea that the drawee's financial obligation was enforceable in court was so accepted in commerce, that court pleadings stopped reciting the details of the original transaction. Does it matter whether the $1000 obligation was created to finance the export of spices or the import of books? Does it matter who the original two merchants were? Once Chase Manhattan Bank has accepted the drafts, thereby admitting that it has an enforceable financial obligation to the holder of the bills, who cares about the original transaction?

This is important because once the financial obligation of the bill became independent of the original commercial transaction, then the holder of the instrument could enforce the obligation free of any defenses or claims presented by the original buyer/borrower. A financial document with this trait is called a "**negotiable**" instrument (not to be confused with the fact that its price or terms were negotiated). Professor Rogers dates negotiability in Anglo-American law to the early 1600s. (The Italians understood negotiability long before, but by the 1600s the action had shifted from the Mediterranean to the Atlantic. Italy's power waned as it was eclipsed first by Spain, and then by England and France).

There are three elements to negotiability. 1) The holder of a negotiable instrument takes title by accepting delivery of an instrument that has been endorsed either directly to the holder or to bearer (endorsed in blank). 2) Consideration is presumed (i.e. the holder is presumed to have paid fair market price for the financial instrument). And 3) the holder takes free of claims and defenses of the original borrower/buyer. This last facet was made possible by divorcing the final financial transaction from the original commercial one.

Financial negotiability revolutionized financial transaction because the holder of such an instrument has better title than the original lender! While the original lender could be sued using a host of claims and defenses, the holder of a negotiable instrument cannot. Financial negotiability, therefore, turns a financial instrument understood only by merchants or legal experts into instruments that is acceptable by everyone. **Negotiability is the mechanism by which paper as a store of value can become bearer instruments acceptable by everyone, such as bearer stock certificates, bearer bonds, bearer notes, checks, paper money, and lottery tickets.**

I don't think that it is coincidence that paper money (a bearer instrument), bearer bonds, and bearer stock, all emerged around the same time that the mechanics and concepts of negotiability became enforceable. A bearer instrument is a paper medium reflecting an underlying financial obligation that is assignable by being endorsed to bearer, and acceptable to all comers due to the protection created by negotiability.

Paper money developed in the 1600s, over three hundred years after Marco Polo first described its use in China. At first, large merchant banks issued notes against their holdings of gold. The problem was that without government oversight, banks could issue more notes than the total value of gold in its vault. It didn't take long for governments to realize the beauty of this scheme and over the next two centuries, printing paper money became a sovereign power of the state. Sweden is credited with issuing the first paper money in 1661, and the idea spread throughout Europe. In the 1690s, the Colony of Massachusetts began printing money; within two decades each of the thirteen colonies was printing its own notes. From the moment of its inception, the U.S. government had a love-hate relationship with central banking. The colorful history of that relationship is the subject of many books and much scholarship. For our purposes, it is only important to note that central banking finally became institutionalized and finalized in 1913 with the creation of the Federal Reserve Bank which has sole authority to print paper money.

In parallel to the development of paper money, paper checks evolved as the main means of payment. In reality, a check is a bill of exchange payable on site. It is an order from one person to his/her bank to pay to the order (instructions) of another person – usually to their bank. The only difference between a check and a bill of exchange is the term; i.e. a check is always payable immediately, while a bill of exchange is payable in the future. (As opposed to Italian custom, by the 1600s English commerce allowed Bills of Exchange to be denominated in the same currency as the original transaction).

During those 250 years in which paper money transformed from unwanted specie to the main media for currency, the doctrines of negotiability and bearability spread to other classes of financial instruments. In the U.S., bearer bonds were probably first issued after the Civil War. They were very popular for several reasons. Since they are not registered, they were very popular for evading taxes and for laundering money. Bearer instruments are also popular among populations that have to flee for their lives, though that was never a reason for its use in the U.S. They might also have been popular in pre-Modern Europe as a means to circumvent the ban on usury, though that is hard to prove.

Another bearer instrument is the negotiable stock certificate. Some credit the Dutch firm Vereenigde Oostindische Compagnie with issuing the first paper stock certificate. While the stock was issued to a named person, the owner could endorse (i.e. sign) the back at which point the stock certificate became a negotiable instrument. In this case it is a bearer instrument. For most of U.S. history, stock certificates were issued to a named buyer. Even if a person bought only one share of stock, the company issued a beautiful, embossed certificate of ownership. Many people would buy one share just to receive that beautiful certificate. I remember receiving stock certificates in my name for a couple of shares of stock on birthdays, and important occasions. The stock broker would always issue a stern warning: Keep them safe or else. (This, of course, was not true since certificates are replaceable; they are the equivalent of cash until reported loss at which point the original certificate is cancelled, the way a check can be cancelled).

Finally - the paper real estate note. A note, which is the debt taken to purchase real estate, is a negotiable instrument. It can be endorsed to a specific party or endorsed in blank. Either way, it is negotiable in that a buyer for consideration receives debt free and clear of any claims or defenses emanating from the original transaction.

To sum up, from the early 1100s through the mid 1900s, paper evolved into a store of value that, combined with the concepts of endorsement, bearability, and negotiability, created several classes of financial instruments including stock certificates, bearer bonds, bearer notes, paper checks, and paper money.

And all that is coming to an end in our lifetime.

The first class to fall was stock certificates. I remember the first time that 50 million shares were traded on the New York Stock Exchange. It was headline news. The year was 1976. Today, fifty million shares can be traded in one company in one hour (as with Facebook, on Oct. 31, 2012). It is not only the sheer volume of trading that makes stock certificates obsolete. It is also the time in which shares are held.

Many traders turn over shares in minutes, even seconds. It would be impossible to issue certificates in a timely fashion, and it is unnecessary. By the late 1960s - when trading started hitting 12 million shared per day - it became clear that the "paper crunch" needed to be solved. At first, trading was halted early on some days, and stopped completely on other days. Over the years, two main solutions were found, and they both involved replacing paper certificates with electronic bookkeeping.

The first solution was to store all paper certificates in a central warehouse, or depository. The New York Stock Exchange was the logical place to start. Then, in 1973, The Depository Trust Company was formed. First, they simply acted as custodian for certificates; then they began electronic bookkeeping to replace the certificates. According to their website, www.dtcc.com "Today, DTCC's depository maintains custody of some 2.5 million different securities valued at more than $28 trillion, including international securities from more than 100 other countries. Each day, many of these securities are traded over and over again, but the trades are recorded by the depository's book-entry accounting system so that no paper certificates have to change hands." According to USA today (May 25, 2010) DTCC held 32 million paper certificates in 1990, and only 1.6 million by 2010.

The other solution was to change state law so that paper certificates would no longer be mandated by law. Forty nine states have now obliged. Only Arizona (and the Territory of Puerto Rico) requires paper stock certificates. Most companies still offer investors the option of a paper certificate. But they now charge a fee which can range from a few dollars to $500 for a Google certificate (that is besides the price of the share.) Funny enough, there are at least two Internet companies that will sell you the paper certificate of one share of stock: www.giveashare.com and www.oneshare.com) What most investors get today is simply a statement from their broker stating that they have purchased the shares, which are issued to a "street name". The broker holds the investor's stock in book-entry form. Investors can also request that the company hold the security in book-entry form. Either way, the paper certificate is eliminated.

The next class to disappear was the bearer bond. The problem here was not only paperwork but tax-evasion. Creating and storing paper certificates was a burden. But a bigger burden was tax evasion. By the early1980s, interest rates had soared to double digits and the temptation to hide this income by holding unregistered bearer bonds was too great for too many Americans. The fact that bearer bonds could be stolen and secreted overseas led to several movies about the theft of bearer bonds, such as Die Hard and Beverly Hills Cop. In 1982, Congress passed the Tax Equity and Fiscal Responsibility Act of 1982 (TEFRA) which denied deductions of federal income tax on interest from bearer bonds. Since the whole point of municipal tax-free bonds is to avoid taxes, investors would shun such instruments. TEFRA effectively eliminated the bearer bond for U.S. investors. (Non-citizens can still buy them).

Cash and checks began to disappear with the advent of the Internet, electronic payments, credit cards and debit cards. While checks use to comprise most of non-cash payments, by 2010, checks comprised only 22% of non-cash payments, according to The 2010 Federal Reserve Payments Study. In 2012, checks were only 15% of non-cash payments. Even the banks themselves don't want to handle the paper checks. While the checks used to be cleared by the Federal Reserve Banks physically (the checks were flown nightly to their destination), now over 99% of all checks are cleared between banks electronically. Banks send images to each other, instead of paper. In 2013 the Social Security Administration stopped sending paper checks. The value of cash transactions is now less than the value of debit card transactions. Paper money is being replaced by plastic.

Paper as a store of value is coming to an end in our lifetime. There no longer is a need for bearer financial instruments whether stock, bond, check, or cash. The shift from analog to digital has eliminated the need for physical financial instruments. The industry actually uses the term "dematerialize" to describe the elimination of paper for bearer instruments. A good parallel exists in the music industry which has shifted from plastic LP records, to CDs, to MP3 files. Not only has the content been transformed from analog to digital, but the actual media has been eliminated. Instead of a plastic disc, music is generated by a digital file containing ones and zeros. So too, has our money been transformed. The information has been digitized, and the financial instruments dematerialized.

Why then is the bearer note still in full use? Why is real estate debt locked out of the modern era? To what end to we still need the bearer note? To evade taxes? No. As a store of value if we have to run for our lives? For sure not. To keep track of note ownership? If digital technology can keep track of millions of shares traded an hour, why can't it keep track of several million real estate notes issued in the course of an entire year? Yes, security pools might not know to which trust a note will be assigned and a blank endorsement might have some use. But how long does it take to endorse the note one more time? Whatever flexibility the banks use to have with blank endorsement has disappeared with the advent of the digital age.

And so I propose that UCC Chapter 3, and the respective state legislatures, abolish blank endorsement of notes.

1) It is obsolete. The modern economy is moving beyond bearer financial instruments.

2) It is confusing –to lawyers. Many times, working at foreclosure mills, attorneys have brought me a bearer note and

asked, who is the owner? (They really should have asked "who is the holder?") I always had fun picking up the note and saying "I am". Anyone holding a bearer note is the Holder of the note. In fact, a thief of a bearer note can enforce it in court, just like the thief of any bearer instrument can treat it as cash.

3) It is confusing – to judges. There are too many foreclosure cases nationwide where the standing of the Holder is in question. Often, this is due to confusion concerning the blank endorsement. Many cases have been thrown out because of sloppiness on the part of the attorneys who show up in court bearing bonds with blank endorsements. Showing a blank bearer note to the court does not prove standing. First of all, the blank endorsement can be overridden by proof of payment and delivery. While, UCC Chapter 3 empowers the Holder of a bearer instrument to enforce it, UCC Chapter 9 was drafted to solve the problem of provenance. When the identity of the holder is ambiguous, the note should be checked for payment and delivery. Secondly, to prove standing the plaintiff must prove that the bearer note was in its possession on the date the complaint was filed. Many attorneys believe that they can show a bearer bond to the court and end the discussion. They are missing the point. The blank endorsement might prove Holding at the time of presentation to the court; it does not prove Holding at the time the complaint was filed. Using blank endorsements to do a run around the law has backfired on many attorneys.

4) It is confusing to the press. Often, in such cases, the press reports that MERS is at fault when the problem was the chain of title of the note. (The fact that MERS is a plaintiff

in a case in which the foreclosing attorney is thrown out of court for lack of standing does not mean that MERS did anything wrong.)

Financial bearability is fading away. When I was shown the blank notes, my final answer to the inquiring lawyers was: contact the client who sent the note. If the client is the servicer, they'll know whom they represent. And if the client is the Holder, they should have a paper trail of payment and delivery. Which is the real point. If the holder of a bearer instrument can be stripped of the note by a paper trail, then the essence of "bearability" has been neutered. As the law now stands, a bearer note is a cash instrument – until the facts show otherwise. Which means it is not really a bearer instrument. For example – would anyone accept a cash bill knowing that it can be taken away if it had passed through the wrong hands? Of course not. And if the bearer note is not really a bearer instrument, why do we still engage in this legal fiction?

My proposal to abolish the bearer note does not mean that I believe negotiability has come to an end. To the contrary, negotiability is a critical component of the modern economy. The U.S. economy, in fact any modern economy, cannot function for even one second without negotiability. Negotiability separates a financial obligation from the underlying commercial transaction. Without negotiability we don't have cash money; or checks; or stocks; or bonds; or any of the financial instruments which underpin modern commerce. What is changing is the mechanics of negotiability. As financial instruments become "dematerialized" from paper, the rules of endorsement, and bearability, become obsolete. But negotiability still applies to financial instruments of the digital world. The shift from analog to digital is a shift in media, not law. The fact that paper is no longer our store of value, does not mean that the main doctrine underpinning our ability to buy and sell financial instruments need to be changed. It means that the mechanics of financial commerce has changed, not the doctrine that enables that commerce.

To sum up: In the days of bearer instruments, when all financial instruments took the form of paper, usually bearer paper, blank endorsement had much value. Bearability, together with the mechanics of negotiability, converted a worthless piece of paper that documented a commercial transaction into a cash instrument. The modern economy would not have been possible without it. But those days are over. All bearer instruments will soon be gone with the wind. Bearer notes need to be abolished too. They confuse investors, the courts, the press and the public. Blank endorsement no longer serves any purpose. Let us do away with it.

IV. ABOLISH FORECLOSURE REVERSALS AND PUNISH THE GUILTY.

Starting in 2008, the economic recession combined with the escalating decline in real estate values to trigger a national financial freefall and a tsunami of foreclosures. The financial collapse was stopped in time, but the foreclosure crisis continues. Today we stand at an equally precarious point in time, not because of the foreclosure freeze, but because of the threat of foreclosure reversals. In the wake of the admittedly wholesale violation of legal procedures in the foreclosure process, courts are beginning to reverse foreclosures and are threatening to evict buyers of foreclosure property. The possibility even exists that prior owners will regain their property mortgage free!

Scott and Susan Christensen of Poway California have not been evicted from their house — which was already foreclosed — because of improperly notarized documents among other deficiencies.[1] In Fall River, Massachusetts, Mark and Tammy LaRace were allowed to move back into the house from which they were evicted two years earlier. The case is under appeal.[2]

---

[1] Curt Anderson, *Despite Foreclosure Halt, Mortgage Crisis Not Over*, ASSOCIATED PRESS (Oct. 12, 2010 3:40 PM EDT), http://hosted.ap.org/dynamic/stories/U/US_FORECLOSURE_FREEZE_BUSINESS_AS_USUAL?SITE=TXDAM&SECTION=HOME&TEMPLATE=BUSINESS.html

[2] Kathleen M. Howley, Foreclosure *Errors May Cloud Ownership of U.S. Homes*, BUSINESSWEEK (Oct. 1, 2010, 6:37 PM EDT), http://www.businessweek.com/news/2010-10-01/foreclosure-errors-may-cloud-ownership-of-u-s-homes.html

Foreclosure expert Neil Garfield writes: "Millions of people who THINK they have lost their homes still own them."[3] If the courts follow through with their threats, then all foreclosed property will become unmarketable. Who would buy a foreclosed property knowing that they can be evicted? As Ron Lieber writes in the New York Times: "Are you out of your mind to even consider buying a foreclosed property right now?"[4] And if foreclosed property becomes unmarketable, then hundreds of billions of dollars of real estate will be wiped off the books of the nation's financial institutions, thereby restarting the financial freefall by wiping out the equity of even the largest banks. One of the casualties will be the title insurance industry, which will not be able to handle the avalanche of claims made against foreclosed property. A much greater danger is a capital markets freeze-up as the pool of marketable assets is decimated. All of this can be avoided by taking an equitable and balanced approach to the problem of procedural fraud in foreclosure, cutting off this chain reaction before it becomes unstoppable. Three problems to be solved are 1) protecting the innocent; 2) drafting a remedy that is proportionate to the damage; and 3) evaluating the risk to the various players.

The key to stopping foreclosure fraud from triggering another financial collapse is to protect the bona-fide-purchaser-for-value from the consequences of a foreclosure reversal. Since the bona-fide-purchaser-for-value did no harm, he should not be vulnerable

[3] Ellen Brown, *Shock Therapy For Wall Street: JPMorgan Suspends 56,000 Foreclosures, GMAC And BoA Many More*, RENSE.COM (Oct. 2, 2010), http://www.rense.com/general92/shock.htm

[4] Ron Lieber, *Your Money: Avoid Foreclosure Market Until the Dust Settles*, NEW YORK TIMES (Oct. 15, 2010), http://www.nytimes.com/2010/10/16/your-money/mortgages/16money.html?_r=2

to eviction. On the contrary, the bona-fide-purchaser-for-value needs to be encouraged to buy foreclosed properties, invest in them and raise their value. Whatever damages the court wishes to award the previous owner must be paid by the perpetrator of the damage, namely the lender and not by the new owner. State legislatures must grant statutory protection to the bona-fide-purchaser-for-value; otherwise we will witness a total collapse of the foreclosure after-market. While today, the foreclosed owner has one year to bring a suit for fraud, that right should be limited to bringing a suit against the lender. The bona-fide-purchaser-for-value should enjoy a statutory umbrella.

This is not to say that the bona-fide-purchaser-for-value will be protected from any of the other dangers present in the foreclosure process, such as superior claims, unnamed junior claims, unnamed parties of interest, or any of the other myriad pitfalls currently found in buying foreclosed property. The statutory protection suggested here is aimed solely at protecting the bona-fide-purchaser-for-value from a foreclosure reversal due to lender fraud. Punishment must be meted out to the perpetrator, i.e. the lender, and not to third parties who are actually acting in a beneficial manner. The remedy must not hurt the innocent, and must not cause even greater damage than the original fraud.

If fraud in the foreclosure process cannot be remedied by foreclosure reversal, then what remedy is available and advisable? A useful distinction in law distinguishes between procedural and substantive aspects of the law. Foreclosure fraud can be classified accordingly. Fraudulent acts in the foreclosure process such as falsely swearing to personal knowledge of the facts, or notarizing signatures without actual acknowledgment of the signer, are violations of the law. They are unethical and should be punished. But what are the actual consequences of this fraud? If the lender truly owns the note, then the procedural fraud simply bought several weeks of time for the lender, and nothing more. The foreclosed owner lost several weeks, or months, of free rent, but nothing more substantial since the owner still had the right to save the property up till the day of sale, and ten, or twenty days beyond (depending on the state). The remedy should not be foreclosure reversal but rather, compensation for the several weeks or months in which the process was cut short. A limited and capped fine of several thousand dollars might be the right proportion for the damage incurred.

However, if the foreclosure plaintiff cannot prove ownership of the note, then the plaintiff committed both substantive fraud and theft. The lender in this case seized property to which it had no right. It claimed standing when none existed. It evicted owners against whom it had no claim. Severe penalties are in order. It is not enough to reimburse the evicted owners with the value of the lost property. Only double, or even triple damages, would make the foreclosed owners whole and serve as a deterrent against bringing suit to foreclosed property pledged to others.

Unbelievably, there have been calls from important economic voices to allow mortgage servicers the right to foreclosure without documentation. This is unconscionable and flies in the face of centuries of legal doctrine. The whole point of title is that if you can't prove title, you don't have title. This is true with ownership and is equally true with liens and encumbrances. There is absolutely no justification to rewarding sloppy institutions that ignored basic procedures when conveying real estate documentation. Any institution that cannot prove ownership of the mortgage, whether by producing the original or submitting a complete chain of assignment, has no standing to foreclose. (Many pundits, economists, and

Congressmen are challenging the legitimacy of MERS, but that is a different matter[5],[6].)

The third leg of this plan involves re-evaluating underwriting premiums of title insurance. Since the proposed statute would eliminate foreclosure reversal as a remedy for foreclosure fraud, title insurers would be exposed to less risk when insuring the purchase of foreclosed property. Title insurers should cede to the state that part of the premium which otherwise would cover the costs of foreclosure reversal. It could be argued that the cost of foreclosure reversal is greater than the entire premium. (Actually it might be greater than the entire equity of the all title underwriters since the courts could reverse one million foreclosures just in 2010). Nevertheless, some part of the premium should be ceded to the state to cover the costs of foreclosure reversals where the lender is bankrupt. It is only fair that if the state reduces the risk to the underwriter, that the underwriters share some of the risk premium with the state. The state would use that premium to cover damages ordered against bankrupt lenders, to cover claims that cannot be covered by illiquid title underwriters, and for administering this program.

To summarize: The real danger lies not in evaluating the extent of foreclosure fraud, but in using foreclosure reversal as a remedy for that foreclosure fraud. Should the courts make foreclosure reversal the common remedy for foreclosure, the market for foreclosed property will collapse, wiping out hundreds of billions of dollars of property now owned by the main financial institutions of the country.

---

[5] Floyd Norris, *Some Sand in the Gears of Securitizing*, NEW YORK TIMES, Oct. 19, 2010, at B1.

[6] Christopher Lewis Peterson, *Two Faces: Demystifying the Mortgage Electronic Registration System's Land Title-Theory*, REAL PROP. PROB. & TR. J. (forthcoming), *available at* SSRN: http://ssrn.com/abstract=1684729.

Such a collapse might bring down the housing market, the capital markets, and even the entire economy. To avoid such a chain reaction, it is recommended that the legislature provide statutory protection to the bona-fide-purchaser-for-value of foreclosed property, but only in terms of foreclosure reversal subsequent to foreclosure fraud. Secondly, a limited, and capped, fine of several thousand dollars should be levied for procedural fraud in the foreclosure process, while substantive fraud should be punished by double, or triple damages. Finally, title insurers should forfeit that part of the premium equal to the risk of foreclosure reversal, since that risk would be eliminated by statute. The state would use that premium to cover damages ordered against bankrupt lenders, to cover claims that cannot be covered by illiquid title underwriters, and for administering this program. By protecting bona-fide-purchaser-for-value, pegging punishments to actual damages, and correctly evaluating the risk premium, we can stop foreclosure reversal from acting as a catalyst of asset liquidation, bank failure and economic catastrophe.

V. A TITLE ANALYSIS OF MERS LITIGATION: THREE AREAS OF NATION-WIDE LITIGATION

Three title issues concerning MERS have been litigated across the United States, in state court and in federal court in almost all of the fifty states.

1) Can MERS execute an assignment of mortgage to assign its title in the mortgage? Alternately, in Title-Theory states: Can MERS execute an assignment of a deed-of-trust to assign its title, and can MERS change the Trustee?

2) Can MERS be a Plaintiff in:

   a. a foreclosure action?
   b. a request for Relief from Stay in a Bankruptcy action?

3) Is the MERS model, which eliminates recording fees for assignments of mortgage, illegitimate (or even illegal) in terms of the duties and rights of the Clerks of Court in the various counties of the fifty states?

While MERS cases are still being litigated in many courts across the country, the results are now clear and the drama has pretty much played out. In this section of the book, the three areas of litigation are summarized and resolved as follows:

1)   All Lien-Theory states recognize MERS' right to execute assign-ments of mortgages. All Title-Theory states recognize MERS' right to assign deed-of-trusts and (except for Washington) to appoint new Trustees. (Cases from States that accepted the MERS model in all of its facets are discussed in **Appendix A.**) In addition, we discuss those states that challenge MERS' title interest by declaring that MERS can assign mortgagers but is not a necessary party of interest in foreclosure. I believe that those state courts are mistaken. Federal courts challenged the state courts on this point.

2)   All states recognized MERS standing when initiating foreclo-sure cases and when requesting relief-of-stay in bankruptcy courts. All states, except for New York, Maine and Vermont rec-ognized that standing by virtue of agency. Those three states, however, did declare that MERS could foreclose as Holder of the note. Important cases from these three states are dis-cussed in **Appendix B**. In the event, this is now academic. As of July 22, 2011 members can no longer foreclose in the name of MERS.

3)   To date, all attacks by the various clerks of court on the MERS system have failed in court. Most notably, Suffolk County in New York was rebuffed on appeal after initial victory in the lower court. As of mid 2013, all county clerks have failed in their actions against MERS.

It should be noted, though, that MERS is involved in other litigation. Across the country, in the various states, and in the various jurisdic-tions, an endless number of accusations have been made in com-plaints against MERS. I don't feel the need to analyze these allegations for several reasons. 1) The fact that an identical list - of 10 to 12 alleged violations - shows up in case after case across the country means that someone's master list is being mindlessly copied. 2) In addition, it seems that foreclosure defense attorneys feel that American law is one giant fishing pond in which to trawl for nasty debris to throw at MERS. There's always something new being dug up, to no avail. 3) I have not found even one case in which the court found MERS to be in violation of any of these laws. 4) Most importantly, since these allegations do not address any issue concerning title, they are not really relevant to this manual. Here is a partial list of the alleged misdeeds of MERS, and laws that MERS is accused of violating, none of which has ever been proven:

Bad Faith	HOEPA – Home Ownership and Equity Protection Act
Breach of Assumed Duty	Misrepresentation (fraudulent and negligent)
Breach of Good Faith & Fair Dealing	Negligence
Civil Conspiracy	Quiet title
Conspiracy to commit fraud	RESPA
Collusion	Slander of title
Deceptive Trade Practices	State Consumer Protection Law
Emotional distress	TILA (Truth in Lending Act)
Fair Housing Act	Unjust enrichment
Federal Consumer Protection Laws	Unfair debt collection
Fraud	Unfair lending
Fraud in the Inducement	Wrongful foreclosure

In addition, several attorney generals, such as Attorney General Martha Coakley of Massachusetts and Attorney General Eric T. Schneiderman of New York have filed actions against MERS in 2012, alleging fraud and deception. New York settled for $25 million. In *State of Delaware v MERSCORP Inc. and Mortgage Electronic Registrations Systems Inc., Delaware Court of Chancery, no. 698*, the State of Delaware alleged violation of Delaware's Deceptive Trade Practices Act. In July 2012, MERS and the State of Delaware signed an agreement. The main point forbids MERS from filing as plaintiff in a foreclosure. This seems to be an unnecessary victory for the State of Delaware since the previous July, MERS issued a prohibition, forbidding its members from filing foreclosure in the name of MERS.

In sum, these actions are a distraction to the real issues presented in this book, namely the title components of MERS, notes and mortgages. While there is an urgent need to clean up the execution of the MERS model (see Chapter II: Clean Up MERS), that cleanup concerns the **execution** of the MERS model, not the MERS model itself.

In the next three sections, the three areas of litigation concerning title are discussed and resolved.

1. MERS and ASSIGNMENTS OF MORTGAGE: MERS WINS

Since MERS holds title to all of the mortgages in its system, at some point it must execute an assignment of mortgage or a release of mortgage. Assignment are needed when the latest holder is not a member of MERS or if the mortgage is being foreclosed. Releases are needed when the mortgage is paid off. Whatever the reason, every mortgage in the MERS system has to eventually be assigned back to the concurrent Holder of the note or released of record. While some early cases, especially in New York, did not recognize MERS' assignments, today all states recognize assignments by MERS. Appendix A discusses the main cases in the various states. Appendix B covers New York which took extra pains to grapple with these issues.

The bottom line is that all states now recognize assignments and releases executed by MERS. Legal recognition of MERS' assignments is based on MERS being the mortgagee-in-title. Of course, the courts don't use that term (coined in "MERS, Notes and Mortgages") but that is what they mean. The courts quote the basic boilerplate language which is found in all MERS mortgages:

""MERS" is Mortgage Electronic Registration System. MERS is a separate corporation that is acting solely as a nominee for Lender and Lender's successors and assigns. **MERS is the mortgagee under this Security Instrument".**

The last seven words, in bold, are the critical words in term of assignment. The mortgage, which is a security instrument drafted as a contract, establishes MERS as the mortgagee. In the tutorial, we discussed the problem with this word. For 450 years "mortgagee" meant the party to whom the property is pledged in case of default. Perforce, that party was the party that received the funds generated by a foreclosure. MERS split "mortgagee" into two parts. While the lender continues to be the party that receives the funds in a foreclosure (since the lender is the mortgagee-in-equity), MERS is the named owner of record of the mortgage. (As noted in the tutorial, the instrument should have named MERS as "mortgagee-in-title", not as "mortgagee"). We know this because of the second boilerplate paragraph found in all MERS' mortgages:

"Borrower understands and agrees that MERS holds only legal title to the interests granted by Borrower in this Security Instrument....."

These words modify the declaration that "MERS is the Mortgagee". In sum, these two statements are unequivocal. MERS is the **mortgagee,** but only holds **title** to the mortgage. The consequence is that when the time comes to transfer title back to the Holder of the note, MERS can, (in my opinion - **must)** execute an assignment. All of the various state courts are now in agreement on this point. Some states buttress MERS' power to assign by citing the fact that MERS is also nominee of the lender with the explicit right to release and cancel the mortgage. That extra verbiage, as we shall see, is poorly drafted; and it is unnecessary when discussing assignments of mortgage. There is no need to call on agency law when dealing with assignments; being the record title-holder of the mortgage, in my opinion, suffices.

Instruments in Title-Theory states use parallel verbiage to declare that MERS is the "beneficiary". I believe that it would have been better to call MERS the "beneficiary-in-title" since MERS does not have any beneficial interest in the security instrument.

One possible exception to this result might be the State of Washington, where the Supreme Court said in *Kristin Bain v. Metropolitan Mortgage Group et al* that MERS is not the beneficiary and therefore cannot appoint a new Trustee for the purposes of foreclosure. (Of course, the lender can do that in any case.) But the court then confused everyone by stating that it is unable to determine the legal effect of this pronouncement. More importantly, the court did not state that MERS cannot assign title to the beneficial interest.

Another problem that MERS faces is the curious situation where states accept MERS' assignment, but declare that MERS is not a necessary party to the transaction. The consequence would be that MERS does not have to be named in a foreclosure action. I believe that those courts do not understand the title interest that MERS has in the security instrument. This is discussed in the next section.

a. State Courts that Mistakenly Held that MERS is Not a Necessary Party –Landmark and its Aftermath

Courts in several states have held that MERS is not a necessary party in a foreclosure action. This can happen, for instance, when the lender is foreclosing and serves the lender of a junior mortgage held by MERS, without serving MERS. This is more serious than it sounds because in order to reach the conclusion that MERS is not a real party of interest, the court must reject the concept that MERS holds title to the mortgage. Those courts are mistaken for two reasons.

1) When the instrument names MERS as mortgagee of the mortgage, then MERS has a **real interest in property.** The owner on title is a party of interest. This has been the case for at least a thousand years. Would those same courts ignore the trustees of trusts in which the beneficiaries disclaim any interest in the property? Of course not. Any court that determines that MERS is not a necessary party, ignores the owner in title of the asset; the asset being the security instrument acting as collateral for the note.

2) Secondly, one of the underlying reasons for splitting title from equity is to differentiate between the publicly known owner of an asset, and its equitable owner. The attraction, or need, for doing this might be legitimate, or illegitimate; that is not relevant to this discussion. What is important is that when such a split in ownership occurs, often, the only way to locate the equitable owner is to use the good offices of the owner in title. In this case, MERS, and only MERS, knows in real time who is the Holder of the note. How can the courts think that justice is done by serving the original lender, when the note might have passed through a thousand hands?

We will demonstrate these points in the following well known cases, in which this mistake was made:

KANSAS

A landmark case concerning MERS is *Landmark National Bank v. Kesler* (2008). The holder of the first note and mortgage, Landmark National

Bank named the Holder of the second note and mortgage, Millennia Mortgage Corp. Millennia didn't answer; a default was entered and the property was ordered to be sold. But Millennia had sold the second note to Sovereign Bank. MERS held title to the mortgage acting as collateral to the note first held by Millennia, and then by Sovereign. An assignment to Sovereign was not recorded since MERS still held title to the mortgage. MERS and Sovereign petitioned the court to reverse the foreclosure, since they had never been served. The court refused, as did the Kansas Court of Appeals. The court claimed that since MERS has no interest in the note, and since, MERS was not given any powers, there was no need to serve MERS.

1) The court's first mistake was concluding that MERS had no interest in the property. As we have explained, being the owner in title has been recognized as an interest in property for over a thousand years. The court did not understand that MERS is the mortgagee-in-title and as such, has a real interest in that collateral asset.

2) Secondly, the court ignored the mechanics of MERS' operations at three different levels.

a. The court states on P. 3 that in the mortgage ".. there is no express grant of any right to MERS to transfer or sell the mortgage, or even to assign its duties as nominee." Surely this is wrong. Every mortgage expressly states that MERS acts as nominee of the lender. But even if this particular mortgage did not, all the court had to do was to review the MERS Membership Agreement to see that every member of the MERS network gives MERS the express right to assign the mortgage.

b. Furthermore, one of the expressed purposes of having a centralized registry is to have an address to serve court papers. If Millennia didn't respond, might it not be that they no longer hold the second note - having sold it to another investor? Since it is the court's obligation to review that all parties of interest are served, why is the court hostile to making inquiry of the MERS registry to find out who does hold the second note? The answer was only a phone call away.

c. Finally, the court ignores the basic MERS model, which is that all members agree to MERS holding title to the mortgage for the purpose of public recording. This way, the note can be sold multiple times without having to run to court each time to record an assignment of mortgage. The court states that serving the lender of record is enough. Wrong! The mortgagee-in-title needs to be served, not the lender of record.

One of the weirder aspects of this case is the following statement made early on: p.2: "No matter the nomenclature, the true role of a party shapes the application of legal principles in this case". Well, the court misread the roles - the role that MERS plays as holder of title to the mortgage, as nominee for the lender, and as a central database to identify Holders of the note.

Many other courts used this mistaken decision to compound the damage. For instance, the Kansas Court of Appeals took the *Landmark* ruling and made it worse in *MERS v. Graham and Martinez*. This is discussed in the section on State v. Federal jurisdiction below.

ARKANSAS

Another widely cited case is MERS vs. *Southwest Homes of Arkansas* (2009) decision issued by the Supreme Court of Arkansas. In this case, MERS held title as beneficiary of a deed-of-trust with regards to the first mortgage. There was also a second mortgage. When payments for the second mortgage stopped, the second mortgagee foreclosed. While the first lender was served, MERS was not served. The property was auctioned. MERS sued for relief arguing that it was a necessary party. Relying heavily on the *Landmark* case, the court ruled against MERS stating that MERS is granted no rights as to the property, and has no interest in the property.

1) The court opens with a weird statement: p. 3: "MERS asserts that it held legal title to the property….". And throughout the case, the court keeps repeating that MERs could not obtain legal title. Either counsel for MERS did not understand the subject material, or the court misunderstood their claim. MERS never holds legal title to real property, with the exception – no longer possible – of MERS being issued a certificate of title after a foreclosure in its name, which is not the case here. Of course the court is right that MERS cannot obtain legal title to the property. That is irrelevant. MERS does hold title to the security interest which pledges the property against the note. That is very different than holding title to the property.

2) Secondly, the court misunderstands the MERS model. MERS correctly states that it can act for whoever is the lender at any given time. The court misinterprets these remarks and states: p. 4 "We specifically reject the notion that MERS may act on its own, independent of the direction of the specific lender who holds the repayment". Well, MERS never claimed that it

is acting *independently* of the lender. MERS never acts of its own accord. What MERS was trying to explain to the court is that the note can change hands many times. And MERS can represent whoever is the lender in real-time, not on its own, but by instruction.

3) In some Title-Theory states, both the Trustee and the Beneficiary have the right to initiate foreclosure. When the court states that the power was not conveyed to MERS, it is not clear if the court is stating that in Arkansas only the Trustee can initiate foreclosure, or if it is stating that the Beneficiary can also initiate an action but that MERS is not the Beneficiary. In any case, the discussion is irrelevant because MERS did not request to foreclose in this case. All that it requested was to be served as a party of interest. Since service is a paramount concern in foreclosure, it is hard to understand the court's dismissal of MERS' request. This is especially true if the lender that had been served was no longer the Holder of the note. Since only MERS knows who is the lender in real-time, MERS needs to be served as a necessary party.

4) While the Deed-of-trust names MERS as beneficiary, and authorizes it to act as agent, the court declares: p. 4, "Further, MERS is not the beneficiary, even though it is so designated in the deed-of-trust." One would hope that the court would honor the terms of the contract between the various parties. In addition, the court ignores the fact that the beneficial interest which the lender holds is an asset, and any asset can have its ownership split into title and equity.

To sum up, MERS requested the court to recognize that it is a party of interest as title holder to the beneficial interest created by the deed-of-trust. The court responded with an all-out assault declaring that not only is MERS not a party of interest, it has no rights or powers whatsoever.

An interesting sequel to *Southwest* is *Coley v. Accredited Home Lending, Inc.* In this case, the borrowers claimed that MERS has no right to assign the mortgage. In this case, the court decided that while *Southwest* holds as to MERS not being able to act on its own, nevertheless, MERS has the right to assign the mortgage. The court bases the right of MERS to assign the mortgage on MERS being an agent of the lender. A more correct basis for the right to assign is the fact that MERS is beneficiary-in-title, namely that it hold title to the security interest of the deed-in–trust.

The court does make a basic mistake in claiming that MERS can assign not only the mortgage, but the note too. This is a common mistake, as explained throughout this treatise. MERS cannot assign the note.

It is interesting, though, to examine this court's understanding of the Arkansas Supreme Court in *Southwest*. According to this court, the Arkansas Supreme Court did not accept MERS' claim to being a necessary party of interest, because p. 6: "…it was not reasonable for the agent, MERS, to presume that the principal would want the foreclosure to be set aside." That's an interesting take. And it stirs up an entirely different issue: who exactly was "MERS" in that case? Was it the real MERS from Virginia, or was it the lender acting on its own but using "MERS" as a front? On one hand we know that MERS never acts on its own. We also know that all members of the MERS system could litigate foreclosure in the name of MERS. Was the request in *Southwest* to be named as a party of interest submitted by the lender (using the name MERS) because the lender did not want to walk away from the property? Or did the real MERS step in because it saw that case as a threat to its business model? After all, the court determination that MERS has no real interest could undermine the entire MERS system of holding title to the security interest of 70 million real estate transactions. I hope that the court in that case knew the answer. We the public will never know.

INDIANA

An interesting situation appears in *Citimortgage v. Barabas* (2011). In this case, the lender of the second mortgage foreclosed its loan. In the process it served the lender of the first loan, but did not serve MERS which was the named as mortgagee in the mortgage instrument. The lender of the first mortgage disclaimed any interest in the property. MERS subsequently assigned the mortgage to Citimortgage, which tried to reverse the foreclosure. Citimortgage claimed that MERS, as a party of interest, had not been noticed in the action. The court decided to follow the Kansas decision in *Landmark* and denied Citimortgage's request. The court stated: P. 11: "Thus, when Irwin Mortgage filed a petition and disclaimed its interest in the foreclosure, MERS, as mere nominee and holder of nothing more than bare legal title to the mortgage, did not have an enforceable right under the mortgage...". Indeed, "mere nominee" sounds pretty worthless until you realize that the right to foreclose is specifically assigned to MERS. Furthermore, as title owner, MERS was the **only** party that needed to be served with notice. Given the fact that the note can be sold many times a day, only MERS could possibly know who was the Holder of the note at the time of service. Why did it not occur to the court that the first lender disclaimed any interest because it no longer Held the note? Once MERS is served, there would have been no need to serve the original lender. If the original lender had still been the Holder, MERS would have forwarded the court papers to them. If not, and such obviously was the case, MERS would forward the papers to the correct party. By ignoring the fact that MERS held legal title to the mortgage, and manages the database of who Holds what note, the court inflicted an injustice on the Holder of the note.

Next, we will discuss how a Federal court ruling on a different problem, fixed the mess made by *Landmark*.

b. MISSOURI: How the Federal Court Used Bellistri to Fix Landmark

A Federal Court made it clear that MERS is a party of interest; and that MERS' right to notice is protected by the Constitution of the United States. This was during an appeal of a nationally watched case on a different subject.

In *Bellistri v. Ocwen Loan Servicing, LLC.* (ED 91369), Robert Bellistri bought a tax certificate for a property in which the owner did not pay taxes for three years (2002, 2003, and 2004). The original lender for the purchase of this property was BNC Mortgage, which received a deed-in-trust with MERS named as beneficiary and nominee of BNC Mortgage. In May 2006 Bellistri sent BNC Mortgage a letter stating that it had 90 days to exercise the right to redeem the property. BNC Mortgage did not answer since it had sold the note back in 2002 to a trust for which Deutsche Bank National Trust Company served as trustee. Ocwen Loan Servicing serviced the trust. Neither MERS, nor Deutsche Bank, nor Ocwen were notified of the impending tax deed. In 2006, the Collector of Revenue for Jefferson County issued a collector's deed to Bellistri. In Dec. 2006 Bellistri filed a quiet title action (in which Ocwen was served). At this point, MERS assigned the deed-of-trust to Ocwen. In April 2008, the Circuit Court of Jefferson County granted Bellistri's motion for summary judgment to quiet title.

In March 2009 the Missouri Court of Appeals affirmed. Incredibly, the court wrote: p. 5 "While Ocwen is the recorded grantee of the assignment of the deed-of-trust, it has no legally cognizable interest." The court explains on p. 6: "When it assigned the deed-of-trust, MERS attempted to transfer to Ocwen the deed-of-trust "together with any and all notes and obligations therein described or referred to, the debt respectively secured thereby and all sums of money due and to become due". The record reflects that BNC was the holder of the promissory note. There is no evidence in the record or the pleadings that MERS held the promissory note or that BNC gave MERS the authority to transfer the promissory note. MERS could not transfer the promissory note; therefore the language in the assignment of the deed-of-trust purporting to transfer the promissory note is ineffective......MERS never held the promissory note, thus its assignment of the deed-of-trust to Ocwen separate from the note had no force". The court concludes: p. 7 "As Ocwen holds neither the promissory note, nor the deed-of-trust, Ocwen lacks a legally cognizable interest and lacks standing to seek relief from the trial court". How many mistakes did the court make?

1) "There is no evidence in the record or the pleadings that MERS held the promissory note". MERS never holds the note except, in certain cases before July 22, 2011 when the note was held in blank by a certified officer of MERS. In this case, MERS did not claim to hold the note.

2) "...or that BNC gave MERS the authority to transfer the promissory note." MERS never claimed to transfer the note. The note was conveyed by BNC to Deutsche Bank as Trustee for the certificate holders of a trust. Lenders *never* give MERS authority to transfer the note. The note is conveyed by payment, endorsement and delivery.

3) Furthermore, MERS does not execute the assignment of the security interest. The lender, or an agent of the lender

executes the assignment by having one of its employees who is a "certified officer" of MERS sign the assignment.

4) True, the verbiage of the assignment of the deed-of-trust is misleading in that it purports to assign the note also. There are millions of such poorly drafted assignments across the country – in every single county of the nation. The judge should have known that verbiage purporting to assign the note was superfluous, and irrelevant. Notes are not conveyed by assignment of the security interest when MERS is involved.

5) "MERS never held the promissory note, thus its assignment of the deed-of-trust to Ocwen separate from the note had no force". Wrong. Ocwen was the servicer for the entity that already held the note – Deutsche Bank (as trustee). The MERS assignment simply reunited title of the deed-of-trust with ownership of the note.

It is incredible to me that the attorney for Ocwen could not explain the mechanics of MERS, notes and mortgages to the judges. Equally astounding is that the court made such basic mistakes. More astounding is that this case was picked up by the press, and by legal scholars as an example of how MERS was going down. Professor Peterson in a nationally publicized paper: "Two Faces: Demystifying the Mortgage Electronic Registration Systems' Land Title-Theory" (Trust and Estate Law Journal 9/29/10) seized on this case as one of several that p. 10 "..have cracked the edifice of Janus-masked façade of MERS-recorded mortgages and deed-of-trust." Prof. Peterson's paper received nationwide attention, including coverage by the New York Times.

A popular toy, and art form, in Russia is a set of five to ten dolls in which each one fits into the next larger size. The Missouri Court of Appeals' decision in *Bellistri* can be compared to such Russian Dolls.

First, an authorized agent for MERS drafts, executes and records an absurd instrument. Secondly, the attorney for MERS fails to set the record straight. Third, the Missouri Court of Appeals uses that defective instrument to draw an incorrect conclusion. Fourth, legal scholars misinterpret the meaning of the case.

In the event, in 2010, a Federal Court overturned Bellistri. The United States District Court for the Eastern District of Missouri (No. 4:09 CV-731 CAS) cancelled Bellistri's tax deed for several reasons. First, Missouri law mandates that a tax deed cannot be issued unless everyone having a "claim upon that real estate" is notified, and MERS, which held a publicly recorded interest, was not notified. Secondly, and most importantly, MERS as nominee for the lender has the constitutionally protected right to due process (Fourteenth Amendment). Third, p.23 "MERS has the right to file suit to foreclose the mortgage…". Finally, p. 23 "The deed-of-trust also gives MERS the right to enforce the lien on the property via a power of sale in the trustee".

While I agree with all of the conclusions of this Federal decision I feel that the Federal court never dug down to the nitty-gritty of this transaction. The state court simply did not understand the mechanics of how notes are conveyed, and what assignments accomplish. The Federal court did not set them straight; and this is why I have to write this manual. However, the Federal decision was courageous in declaring that MERS is a party of interest, and in invoking the U.S. Constitution to protect MERS' real interest in property.

2. MERS AS PLAINTIFF IN A FORECLOSURE ACTION: MERS WINS AND SURRENDERS

Up to July 22, 2011, the MERS Membership Agreement allowed lenders to foreclose in the name of MERS. This meant that MERS could be the named plaintiff in foreclosure actions in state courts (since Real Estate Law is under state jurisdiction), and in Motions for Relief from Stay in Federal courts (since Bankruptcy Law is under Federal jurisdiction). This duality is further explored in the next section.

What was the basis for the complaints filed against MERS? The complaints revolved around two different doctrines, which are really related, as follows:

1) First, if MERS does not Hold the note, or have the rights of the Holder, on what basis can it bring an action to enforce the note? All states have adopted UCC Paragraph 301 which defines who may enforce a note:

§ 3-301. PERSON ENTITLED TO ENFORCE INSTRUMENT.

> *"Person entitled to enforce"* an instrument means **(i) the holder of the instrument,** *(ii) a* **nonholder in possession of the instrument who has the rights of a holder,** *or (iii) a person not in possession of the instrument who is entitled to enforce the instrument pursuant to Section 3-309 or 3-418(d). A person may be a person entitled to enforce the instrument even though the person is not the owner of the instrument or is in wrongful possession of the instrument.*

("MERS Notes and Mortgages" discusses the various components and mechanics of the negotiable note and mortgage.) If MERS is initiating an action which should be prosecuted by a different party, then that would be a violation of the doctrine of Prudential Standing. Standing cannot be waived and can be challenged by any party at any time. It is critical to the due process of law. If lack of standing is proved, then the certificate of title issued at the end of a foreclosure can be vacated.

2)   Secondly, since MERS suffers no loss, then it is not a Party-of Interest. Rule 17 of the Federal Rules of Civil Procedure reads as follows:

> 17(a)(1) "..an action must be prosecuted in the name of the real party in interest."

Complaints against MERS claimed that since MERS has no interest in the note, it loses nothing and should therefore be precluded from initiating a foreclosure action.

While these seem to be two different doctrines, many courts dealing with MERS explain the following. There are two tests for standing. The first criterion is called Constitutional standing which comes from Article III of the Constitution. Constitutional standing is the requirement that (*In re Joshua and Stephanie Mitchell p.4*) "....a party must have suffered some actual or threatened injury as a result of the defendant's conduct, that the injury be traced to the challenged action, and that it is likely to be redressed by a favorable decision." In short, there must be "injury in fact, causation, and redressibility". The second criterion is called Prudential standing "...which is judicially-created set of principles that places limits on the class of persons who may invoke the courts' powers". It turns out that "Party-of-Interest" is really one of the tests of Prudential Standing.

Why then was MERS attacked differently in different jurisdictions? The difference goes back to the difference between Lien-Theory and Title-Theory discussed in Chapter 12 of the Tutorial. In Lien-Theory states, a foreclosure action is an action to enforce the note. So in those jurisdictions, a complaint against MERS would naturally start with the UCC 3-301 issue of MERS not being the Holder of the note. Federal Rule 17 would come afterward to bolster the complaint against MERS. But in Title-Theory States, a foreclosure action is not an enforcement of the note. On the contrary, all Title-Theory states have declared that there is no necessity to show the note or even be in possession of the note. In Title-Theory states, a foreclosure action is an exercise of the power of sale which was granted by the borrower in the Deed-of-Trust. So UCC3- 301 has no bearing there. But Federal Rule 17 does have bearing; if MERS has suffered no loss, how can it initiate the foreclosure action?

Both State and Federal courts resolved both sets of issues on the basis of agency law.

1) As to Federal Rule 17, the problem is solved by the last part of the rule which states: "The following may sue in their own names without joining the person for whose benefit the action is brought……..a party with whom or in whose name a contract has been made for another's benefit.". Since MERS clearly is in contract to act for the benefit of the lender, MERS has standing in non-judicial foreclosure.

2) As to UCC 3-301, most state legislatures, when integrating UCC 301 into their codes, modified the right to enforce by stating that the note can be enforced by the Holder of the note, "or its agent". Those three words are critical. Once again let's look at the boilerplate language found in every MERS mortgage:

""MERS" is Mortgage Electronic Registration System. **MERS is a separate corporation that is acting solely as a nominee for Lender and Lender's successors and assigns**. MERS is the mortgagee under this Security Instrument".

This time we emphasize the second sentence which declares that MERS is nominee for the Lender. Nominee is defined as a limited agent; an agent who is empowered with a few, very specific, powers.

Courts combined that paragraph with the following verbiage found in every MERS mortgage:

"Borrower understands and agrees that MERS holds only legal title to the interests granted by Borrower in this Security Instrument, **but if necessary to comply with law or custom, MERS (as nominee for Lender and Lender's successors and assigns) has the right: to exercise any or all of those interests including, but not limited to, the right to foreclose and sell the Property**; and to take any action required of Lender including, but not limited to, releasing and canceling this Security instrument."

In other words, the security instrument declares that MERS is the limited agent of the lender ("nominee") and then MERS is assigned the "right to foreclose". This combination has led most courts to accept MERS as plaintiff in both foreclosure cases and requests for relief from stay. As a side note, Minnesota adds a second reason for allowing MERS to foreclose. According to Minnesota law, the holder of title to the mortgage can foreclose by virtue of being the mortgagee of record. This was legislated by the Minnesota legislature. I don't believe that any other state would accept MERS standing to litigate simply on its holding title to the security instrument. All other states, except Maine, Vermont and New York, justify MERS standing by referring to its assigned powers as nominee.

Of course, there were states such as Florida which based the right of the lender to foreclose in the name of MERS on some connection to the note. As discussed in Chapter 15 of the Tutorial, all such legal theories are flawed. MERS is concerned with the security instrument, not the Note.

Another side issue: Many courts have questioned, in bewilderment, the phrase "if necessary to comply with law or custom". The phrase creates ambiguity: Since it is not "necessary" (e.g. MERS can always assign the mortgage back to the lender) does MERS ever really have this power? Even worse, does this modify MERS' power to assign? Different courts have interpreted this verbiage in different ways. For our purposes, suffice it to say that most courts did not let the poor drafting distract from the real issues here.

Three states did not accept foreclosure actions initiated in the name of MERS, namely New York, Vermont and Maine. In all three states, the courts demanded a strict reading of UCC 3-301. Accordingly, in those three states, the party empowered with enforcement of the note is the actual Holder – and not the agent of the Holder. The main cases from these states are discussed in Appendix B. However, courts in all three states were unambiguous in stating that foreclosure could be initiated in the name of MERS if MERS is the Holder of the note. And this mechanism was available to lenders before July 22, 2011. In sum, MERS won the right to foreclose in every state where the issue was litigated, either as agent of the Holder, or as Holder itself.

But, as explained, this victory was pyrrhic. MERS surrendered the flag unconditionally by stopping foreclosure in its name on July 22, 2011. Why? MERS litigated this issue in at least 38 states. Thirty five of those states allow MERS to be the plaintiff by virtue of its agency powers. Another three states, New York, Vermont and Maine allow MERS to be plaintiff if it is the Holder of the note. So MERS won every battle, and the war, yet surrendered. Why? Imagine that Ulysses S. Grant and Robert E. Lee enter the Courthouse at Appomattox. Grant hands Lee the terms of surrender. Lee picks up a pen to sign. Just as pen meets paper, Grant says: "Only kidding. You win. The South is independent; we'll go back home". That is not the usual course of events. I believe that the reason for this surrender stems from the fact that there is no added value to having MERS be the plaintiff.

When it comes to MERS privatizing the role of county recorder as far as assignments are concerned, there is value added since both time and money are saved for all parties. But those savings don't exist when MERS is named as plaintiff in a foreclosure action.

1) In Lien-Theory states the plaintiff must prove to the court that it is in possession of the note on the date that the complaint is filed. Any change of plaintiff must be accompanied by correct filings in court. And, in theory at least, MERS should assign out before the sale. So keeping MERS as the mortgagee does not save any paperwork or recording fees. So there are no savings in starting the process in the name of MERS.

2) As for Title-Theory states, the court must be informed of any change of beneficiary. And the plaintiff must be substituted in as Trustee before the sale. Again, there are no savings to anyone by starting the process in the name of MERS.

This wave of litigation was unfortunate. It was costly, unnecessary, and distracted from the more important justification for MERS' existence.

Further analysis of cases from States which accepted the MERS model is provided in Appendix A. Cases from Maine, Vermont and New York are provided in Appendix B. While this wave of litigation is winding down and is basically over, a review of these cases is useful since there is still much to be done to clean up MERS and modernize the American real estate transaction.

NEXT: Two tangential problems are discussed in the next two sections. The first occurs when Federal courts and state courts conflict with each other. The second is the scenario by which MERS purportedly became the Holder of the note in order to obtain standing in foreclosure cases.

a. State Jurisdiction (Foreclosure) vs. Federal Jurisdiction (Bankruptcy)

Real Estate law is considered a local matter, and so it is decided by state law. Each state decides its own real estate law. The courts of each state adjudicate real estate matters including foreclosure. On the other hand, bankruptcy is a federal matter. It is dictated by Federal Law and adjudicated in Federal court.

Why would foreclosure ever be adjudicated in a Bankruptcy proceeding? When a borrower files for bankruptcy, all foreclosure proceedings are halted immediately, by Federal law. One common route taken by lenders is to request a "relief from stay". This means that the court is asked to remove the property that was named in the foreclosure proceedings from the basket of assets which the bankruptcy trustee is safeguarding and evaluating. When it is clear that the sale of the property will not cover the mortgage, then there is no point in selling the asset to pay off debts. If no money can be generated after paying off the mortgage, then why bother to protect this asset? So if the equity has been wiped out, the property is removed from the Trustee's protection. In other words, the Federal court grants a "relief" (i.e. removal) from "stay" (i.e. the freeze imposed on assets belonging to the petitioner for bankruptcy).

In several states, Federal Courts of a given state have made determinations which stand in opposition to the position taken in State Court. Here we discuss Kansas and Nevada. In Kansas the Federal court corrected mistakes made in state court. In Nevada, the state courts correct the Federal courts.

KANSAS

The Kansas Court of Appeals took the *Landmark* ruling (discussed above) one step further in *MERS v. Graham and Martinez*. While *Landmark* determined that MERS is not a necessary party in a foreclosure proceeding, the Court of Appeals interpreted that to mean that MERS has no standing at all as a plaintiff in a foreclosure action. That faulty conclusion is based on both the faulty reasoning of *Landmark*, and on mistakes that this court makes for itself.

1) First, the Court of Appeals repeats the faulty *Landmark* reasoning and states that since MERS has no interest in the note, then MERS has no rights in the security interest acting as collateral for than note.

2) The Court of Appeals then makes its own mistake by stating that p. 10 "…there is no evidence that MERS received permission to act as an agent…" (i.e. for the plaintiff).

3) Finally: "Having suffered no injury, MERS lacks standing to bring a foreclosure action". So the Court of Appeals took a bad decision and made it worse. But the United States Bankruptcy Court for the District of Kansas disagreed.

Martinez and Graham (a common-law couple) declared bankruptcy. MERS requested Relief from Stay. The Federal Court granted MERS request for Relief from Stay and took a stand diametrically opposed to the State Court.

1) First, the Federal Court states that MERS is the holder of title to the mortgage.

2) Secondly, the Federal Court rejected the reasoning of the State Court that since MERS is not a necessary party (per *Landmark*) therefore MERS cannot be plaintiff in a foreclosure action *(per Martinez and Graham)*.

3) The Federal Court actually cites *Landmark* as stating that should MERS be proved to be the agent of the lender, MERS could be a plaintiff in a foreclosure proceeding. And since MERS is the agent of the lender: "…the Court concludes that MERS was clearly acting as an agent for (lender) at all relevant times". (As we noted in our introduction above, MERS never acts on its own accord.) Therefore, the Court concludes, MERS clearly has the right to be plaintiff of the foreclosure action.

So the Federal Court makes a correct determination. It recognizes that since MERS is agent for the Lender, it can be plaintiff in a foreclosure action – contrary to the decision of the state court. However, once the Federal Court recognized MERS to be the title holder of the mortgage it should also have realized that the *Landmark* ruling was faulty too.

In any case, the Federal and State Courts in Kansas maintain different postures vis-à-vis MERS and this demonstrates how the sloppy thinking displayed by MERS has confused the courts and muddied the waters for everyone.

NEVADA

Nevada courts issued decisions similar to courts in the other Ninth District states. In *Orzoff v. MERS*, 2009 WL 4643229 at p. 6 (D. Nev. Mar 2, 2009) "Plaintiff has cited no authority that is controlling upon this Court that holds MERS cannot have standing as a nominee beneficiary in connection with a non-judicial foreclosure proceeding under Nevada Law". In *Vazquez v. Aurora Loans* (D. Nev. Mar. 30, 2009) p.2 the court found that MERS has standing. In *Gonzalez v. Home American Mortgage Corp.* the court found that, like other Title-Theory states, the beneficiary, and the trustee have the right to initiate foreclosure without presenting the note. Finally in *Ramos V. MERS*, Inc., (Mar. 5, 2009) the court held that MERS can appoint a substitute trustee.

So while Nevada state courts saw no problem with MERS assigning the deed-of-trust, or appointing a successor trustee, or foreclosing, the Federal Courts weren't too happy with MERS. *In re Joshua and Stephanie Mitchell* is a review of MERS' requests to lift automatic stay in twenty seven cases. This is a difficult case to analyze, first because counsel for MERS was clearly confused. The court itself points out: p. 5: "It is unclear whether MERS is arguing that It has standing in its own right, or as the agent of the entity entitled to enforce the note, or both". When MERS argues that it has been given authority to act for the beneficial owner of the loan, it stands on sturdy ground. But when MERS states (p.6) that it has the right to act as the note's Holder, then counsel loses credibility since MERS is never the Holder except for certain circumstances (discussed in the Tutorial) which did not occur in this case. It turns out that most of the plaintiffs in whose name MERS was acting, were not really the Holders of the note. The note had been assigned earlier to other parties. Apparently, the wrong lenders were initiating legal action. So this case boils down to a lesson in how not to go to court.

In the Federal court case, *Smith vs. Community Lending, Inc.* the Federal court makes many title mistakes when discussing MERS, notes and mortgages. The court cites the following standard verbiage from the deed-of-trust: "Borrower understands and agrees that MERS holds only legal title to the interests granted by Borrower in this Security Instrument...". P. 2:

1) The court states: "In fact, MERS does not hold legal title, despite the language of the FDOT (First Deed-of-trust)". Wrong. As explained in the Tutorial above, MERS holds title to the security interest.

2) "The trustee holds legal title, which is its function". The court is confusing title to the property with title to the pledge of the property. As explained in the tutorial, a deed-of-trust encompasses two different transactions; the first is the conveyance of land, and the second is the pledging of that land as security. In the first transaction, the borrower conveys title (to the property) to the Trustee. In the second transaction, the borrower agrees that MERS holds title to the pledge of that property.

3) The court correctly states that MERS, "under this deed-of-trust, may initiate a foreclosure." But then the court errs in stating that the powers of the deed-of-trust allow MERS to transfer the note also. The court believes that calling MERS the "beneficiary", together with the language quoted above, "….indicates an intent to give MERS the broadest possible agency on behalf of the owner of the beneficial interest in the underlying debt." That is incorrect. MERS does not have that power. The deed-of-trust only gives MERS powers in terms of the mortgage, not the note.

4) The court compounds this error by stating that "such agency would include the ability to sell the interest in the debt." That clearly is not true. MERS can never sell the note; it does not own the note, does not possess the note, cannot endorse the note, and does not even see the note.

5) While the court commits the errors above, it keeps repeating that "…MERS is not in fact the beneficiary…". As explained

repeatedly in the tutorial above, MERS holds title to the beneficial interest of the security pledge, and as such is the Beneficiary in Title.

6) The court correctly states that MERS can assign the deed-of-trust. Then the court states that the equity in the note would follow along "as a matter of law" and that this proves that MERS assigned the note. Wrong. MERS does not assign the note. The note was negotiated between two banks; MERS' assignment (of the deed-of-trust) followed later.

7) Final mistake: The court concludes that since MERS assigned the note to the plaintiff, the foreclosure is proper. Wrong sequence. The plaintiff already had the note before the MERS assignment was executed. The assignment completed the chain as to the power of sale. That is what made the foreclosure proper.

b. Could MERS Ever Really Be the Holder of the Note?

In the Introduction to this book, we pointed out that one of the four causes of confusion concerning MERS is the misuse of legal fictions. The first fiction allowed lenders to begin foreclosure actions using MERS' name as the plaintiff. How? The security documents declared MERS to be the "nominee" of the lender. "Nominee" in this case meant that MERS was an agent of the lender but only for limited purposes, including the right to foreclose. Since most states allow the Holder "or its agent" to foreclose, MERS won most court battles on this issue. However, the States of New York, Vermont and Maine did not allow foreclosure by an agent of the Holder. So MERS authored a second fiction as follows. MERS gave lenders the option to endorse the note in blank, and transfer it to MERS. The mechanism, as explained before, was to certify a member of the staff of the servicer (or Holder) as an officer of MERS. So when that officer held the note, endorsed in blank, MERS purportedly became the Holder since it was apparently in possession of bearer paper. Due to the immense number of cases litigated across the nation, MERS put a halt to both of these practice as of July 22, 2011 (i.e. foreclosing in the name of MERS, and allowing MERS to be Holder of the note). But it is still important to answer the following questions: Could MERS ever really have been the Holder of the note? We need to answer this question, first in order to understand why courts struggled with this issue. Secondly, the analysis will clarify the relationship between MERS, notes and mortgages.

NORTH DAKOTA

North Dakota– like Florida – is a state that came to the right conclusion based on an incorrect analysis. In *Bray v. Bank of America, et al*, the judge does not master the relationship between MERS, notes, and mortgages. The judge reported, based on two affidavits, that at the time of trial: 1) the note was owned by The Bank of New York Mellon; 2) BAC Home Loan Servicing, LP serviced the note and mortgage and 3) the Vogel Law Firm was custodian of the note and mortgage. A certain Jennifer Guidicessi, claiming to be "Vice President of MERS" testified that:

1) Indeed, The Bank of New York Mellon is p. 4 "the current beneficial owner of the Note".
2) The note was endorsed in blank (making it bearer paper)
3) The note was in possession of counsel for plaintiff.
4) And "…the note is under my control".

Based on all of this information the court made the following determination: p. 10: "The Court finds as a matter of law that MERS owns both the note and the mortgage and thus can foreclose on the real property in question." This is an astounding assertion because, as we have discussed many times before, MERS can never own the note; not in fact, not in law. So the court is clearly confused. Let's discuss why:

1) As repeatedly explained above, MERS can never, legally, be the owner of a note. MERS does not buy notes, invest in notes, or collect payments against notes. The court could have read the MERS Membership Agreement which states that to even claim that MERS owns the note is punishable with a fine of $5,000 for each incident.

2) Even if the court did not understand the legal impossibility of MERS owning the note, it still should have been clear to the court that the Bank of New York Mellon is the owner. The decision itself cites two affidavits stating this very clearly. The first affidavit is from BAC Home Loan Servicing, LP, which sold the note to Bank of New York Mellon, and continued to service the loan. The second affidavit was from the so called "Vice President" of MERS.

3) The court states that (p. 10) "…MERS' possession of the note would give it ownership of the mortgage". Since when does possession prove ownership? For instance, the "non-holder in possession" is never the owner. Or, for instance, the Holder (who by definition must be in possession) might be the owner but not necessarily. The court correctly states that the note was endorsed in blank (making it bearer paper). The note was in possession of the Vogel Law Firm which handed it to their paralegal who was also a MERS "vice president". The court could just as easily, and just as incorrectly, have decided that the Vogel Law firm was the owner, instead of MERS.

4) Furthermore, had the court read the MERS Membership Agreement, it would have understood that upon instruction of the lender, the note can be endorsed in blank, and transferred to MERS for the purpose of foreclosure –in which case MERS becomes the Holder of the note. But how can MERS be the Holder of the note when everyone agrees that BAC Home Loan Servicing, LP is the Holder? The answer is simple. Jennifer Guidicessi is not a real vice president of MERS. She is a "certified vice president". As an employee of the Vogel Law Firm, she can assign the mortgage, and act to foreclose the mortgage, using the title "Vice President of MERS". But she is always acting as an employee of the Vogel Law Firm. The court did not understand that when Jennifer Guidicessi claims that the note "is under my control", what she really meant is that Bank of New York Mellon owns the note, BAC is servicing that note, the Vogel Law Firm is in possession of that note, and MERS is simply being used as a legal fiction.

5) Finally, the court states that as owner, MERS can foreclose. The judge should know that the owner does not have the right to enforce. The Holder has the right to enforce. In order for the owner to enforce, the owner must also be the Holder.

The case is fun to read because of the string of absurdities claimed by the borrower such as the claim that Federal Reserve dollars are worthless. The court does a lot better with the borrower's "frivolous" claims, than it does with the misleading picture painted by counsel for MERS and the lender. While I agree with the court's determination that MERS can foreclose, I disagree with the reasoning of the court.

But even the claim that MERS can be the Holder of the note is problematic. Three states – New York, Vermont and Maine all held that

MERS can only be the plaintiff in a foreclosure action if it is the Holder. **But could MERS ever truly be the Holder of a note?**

In this case, there are actually two parties who can claim, and prove, that they are the Holder of the note. A case can be made that MERS was the Holder of the note. And a case can be made that BAC was the Holder of the note. To review: The Holder of the note is the party that 1) is in possession of the note which is 2) either endorsed in blank, or endorsed to itself.

What is the case for MERS being the Holder of the note? In this case, Jennifer Guidicessi, a "certified" officer of MERS, had the note under her control. And the note was endorsed in blank. Accordingly, MERS was the Holder.

What is the case for BAC being the Holder of the note? "Possession of the note" is not necessarily physical possession. Many notes are held by a "custodian" which is simply a warehouse outfitted to protect these assets from fire, water, or theft. Sometimes the law firms have such safe rooms on premises. Sometimes the work is outsourced to special facilities. When a custodian has possession of the note, the Holder has "constructive possession" which means that it controls the whereabouts of the note, even if it is not on hand. In this case, BAC was in constructive possession of the note. After all, BAC hired the Vogel Law Firm to handle the foreclosure and BAC handed the note to the Vogel law. The Vogel Law Firm acted only upon the instructions of BAC. And MERS was, as it has to be, a passive player. Yes, Guidicessi had the note under her control, but not upon instructions from MERS. Rather, she acted upon instructions of her employer – the Vogel Law Firm which acted on the instructions of BAC.

Here is my solution: **While it might be argued that MERS was the Holder in physical possession, nevertheless, BAC was always**

the Holder in constructive possession. Even if by some stretch MERS is considered Holder due to the possession of the bearer note through its "certified" officer Guidicessi, BAC was always the Holder according to the doctrine of constructive possession. In my opinion, BAC is the real, and only, Holder of the note. Why? Because of the history, and nature, of the construct called "Holder of the note".

Why was this construct – "Holder of the note" – created in the first place? Not every owner wants to be bothered with the work of managing and servicing debt. The richer, or larger, the owner, the less likely that person or entity would be to collect payments, keep track of borrowers, dun them when needed, and foreclose when in default. Think of his Lordship, Earl Robert Crawley of Downton Abbey. Is he going to sully his hands with commerce? All notes due to his Lordship would be signed over to an agent empowered to handle and collect funds. So the Holder is the holder of title to the debt, with actual powers to handle the assets. In sum, the Holder is an **active agent** of the owner.

Bank of New York Mellon is the owner of the note in question. Who is the active agent? BAC, not MERS. MERS is never an active player. MERS never does anything on its own. In fact, MERS never does anything, as it is a passive player which allows its name to be used by its members when executing assignments and satisfactions, and or initiating an action to foreclose. BAC is calling the shots here. BAC is the real Holder because it is also the active agent. It has a better claim on the title of "Holder" than does MERS.

What we really have here are fictions within fictions.

1) The first fiction is that a firm with 50 employees can have 25,000 vice presidents and assistant secretaries.

2) The second fiction is that by handing a bearer note to such a "certified" officer of MERS, who in this case is an employee of the Vogel Law Firm, MERS comes into possession of the note. In fact, no employee of MERS ever comes close to a note, or gains control of a note. There was no delivery to MERS itself. And delivery is a necessary component of being the Holder.

3) The intended consequence of these fictions is the fiction that the status of Holder was transferred to MERS. When a legal fiction creates parallel realities with absurd contradictions, the fiction has been stretched too far. And once you stretch a fiction too far, it snaps. MERS cannot be the Holder of the note when centuries of precedent dictated that BAC, as the active player, was the Holder of the note.

Or to approach the problem from a different angle: In the models presented in "MERS, Notes, and Mortgages", we demonstrated that an asset can have different facets of ownership, especially the well-known separation of title from equity. But can a "power" be broken up into this same set of facets? The Holding of a note is not the ownership of an asset but the acquiring of a power. Can the party holding title to that power be a separate entity from the party actually executing the power? Again, a stretch too far.

Leonardo DiCaprio, in the movie "Inception", plays a character who finds out that when you embed one fiction within another, you can get lost, or even land up in limbo. DiCaprio's character thought he could get away with playing these mind games; but he learned that a return to reality is not always possible and – spoiler alert - sometimes it is not even possible to know when the fiction is over. This is what MERS did when it created the fiction of it being the Holder of the note in order to enable the larger fiction that it was foreclosing on a note. Fortunately, MERS stopped these mind games on July 22, 2011.

Legal fictions are created to serve a purpose; to solve a problem. What problem did MERS solve by allowing lenders to foreclose in its name? None. What purpose was served? None. While MERS' innovation in holding title to the mortgage does serve an economic purpose – it allows the note to be traded without the accompanying delay in recording an assignment of mortgage - there is no purpose in having MERS foreclose or hold title to the note. What is the difference? With mortgages, the public needs to know who is the last lender holding the note and mortgage at the **end** of the process, so that the property, and funds, can be conveyed to the right party. There is no need to know the identity of the interim investors. But with notes, the court needs to know the lender/investor at the time the foreclosure complaint is filed – i.e. at the **beginning** of the foreclosure process. In all Lien-Theory states, the plaintiff in a foreclosure action has to prove that it Holds the note at the time that the complaint is filed. And in Title-Theory states, a beneficiary who is initiating action has to have the assignment of the deed-of-trust recorded in the public records before it starts. If MERS is used as plaintiff for a lender that bought a note that wasn't yet delivered, then the complaint is invalid. The subsequent transfer of the note to the plaintiff lender, or the subsequent recording of the assignment to the beneficiary, does not solve the defect and the foreclosure action must be started all over. Covering up a defective complaint by using MERS as plaintiff does not solve anything. At some point, it must have become clear to MERS, and to its members, that foreclosing in the name of MERS serves no purpose. The multiple fictions at play were not serving any purpose whatsoever. And there's nothing more useless than a legal fiction without a purpose.

3. MERS and CLERKS OF COURT – MERS WINS

Ironically, this topic which is really the most important of all, did not catch fire. One might think that the privatization of a public duty that is hundreds of years old would be challenged in every county in every state of the country. While the MERS system was hard for the title world to digest at the start, it is now an accepted part of the title and real estate universe. I believe that its acceptance can be explained as follows:

There are two reasons to record mortgages in the public record. First, to put all potential purchasers of a given property on notice that a prior lien exists. Secondly, to enable the real estate transaction by informing the purchaser of the name and address of the lien holder so that the lien can be paid off and title cleared. Prior to MERS, these two functions were two sides of the same coin. When you found a lien during a property search, you also found the address to satisfy the lien. By assuming the role of mortgagee-in –title for all mortgages in its system (now over 70 million), MERS eliminated the need to have the name and address of the lender in the public record. All a purchaser of real estate has to do is call the MERS 800 line and information necessary to satisfy the lien (i.e. the name and address of the loan servicer) is immediately available. (In the early years, this system did not work too well and many court cases include criticism of MERS' lack of efficiency in supplying this information. But by now the technical problems have been sorted out. It is several years since I have read of anyone complaining about the MIN lookup system). So while MERS has privatized the information concerning the identification of lenders, the recorded MERS mortgage still gives notice to the public as to the existence of the mortgage. Both functions continue to be fulfilled; one in public, one in private. While the various legislators might never have agreed to this system ab initio, now that the system is working smoothly, and since it does serve a useful economic purpose, it is highly unlikely to be abolished. While MERS does need to be improved and monitored, the American economy would be better served in building on MERS' strengths than on eliminating it just because it gamed the structure of public recording.

New York *Merscorp v. Romaine*. Dec. 19, 2006. This is a landmark case in the history of MERS litigation because it correctly separated the question of the legitimacy of MERS' transactions from its legitimacy in terms of public recording. The judges in this case were clearly conflicted as to whether MERS can be the mortgagee and whether MERS has the right to foreclose. But they did not allow these doubts to escalate into a ban on recording MERS related instruments.

The history of this case goes back to 2001 in which the Attorney General of the State of New York issued an informal opinion stating that the recording of a MERS related instrument violates New York State law concerning real property (particularly Section 316 of Real Property Law) and is contrary to the will of the New York State legislature. As a consequence of this informal opinion, the Clerk of Court for Suffolk County stopped recording MERS related instruments. The Supreme Court for Suffolk County (which is just the highest court in the county, not the state) held that the Clerk of Court must record MERS related mortgages, but does not have to record MERS' assignment-of-mortgages and release-of-mortgages. The Appellate Division Court, in response, found "no valid distinction between MERS mortgages and MERS assignments or discharges for the purpose of recording and indexing" (24 AD3d 673). Finally, the Court of Appeals of New York affirmed those findings.

The first finding, that MERS related mortgages must be recorded is the easier of the two issues to resolve. New York State law is clear. A properly acknowledged and certified conveyance must be recorded by the county clerk (Section 291 of the real Property Law). Real Property Law section 316, which deals only with Suffolk County states that such instruments "..shall be recorded" by the County Clerk. Mortgages do not pose the same problem as assignments and releases since the mortgage states who is the original lender, and that MERS is the nominee for that specific lender. The court points out that it is not the job of the county clerk to worry that in the future, the mortgage instrument will be assigned in a way that is not to its liking. "The Clerk lacks the statutory authority to look beyond an instrument that otherwise satisfies the limited requirements of the recording statute." (It is interesting to note that even the dissenting judge in this case did not have a problem with this finding.) The court even went further and stated it has no problem with MERS being called the mortgagee (P. 5).

The more difficult problem is the recordation of assignments and releases since by the time MERS assigns, or releases the underlying debt, the beneficial interest has usually been transferred one or more times. New York State law requires that the final release be signed by the mortgagee, or the final assignee. The majority and the minority judges in this case argue about the letter of the law as to unrecorded assignments. The majority states that there is no violation of the law since the law allows the final release to simply state that those assignments are not of record. The minority disagrees with that interpretation of the letter of the law and claims that unrecorded assignments must still be listed on the release.

This argument is, with all due respect, irrelevant since, in the MERS system, the beneficial owners of the underlying debt do not execute any assignment of mortgages. This is the whole point of MERS: to avoid having to execute and record assignments. When the majority judges state that the MERS release complies with law by stating that the assignments are not of record, they are missing the point just as badly as the minority judge who demands that all assignments be listed on the final discharge. As long as MERS holds title to the mortgage, no assignments have been made. MERS neither conforms to, nor violates, New York law. MERS makes this statute irrelevant by eliminating the assignment altogether.

In any case, the Court of Appeals of New York State instructed Suffolk County to record all MERS related mortgages, all assignments of mortgage executed by MERS, and all releases of mortgage executed by MERS.

An interesting aspect of this case was a sentence written by the dissenting judge, Judge Kaye, which has been widely quoted across the nation: "It is the incongruity between the needs of the modern electronic secondary mortgage market and our venerable real property laws regulating the market that frames the issue before us." Sums up the problem very well.

Many other clerks of court have attempted to recoup lost recording revenues; all have failed. Here they are in alphabetical order.

Arkansas. The clerk of court for Hot Spring County, Arkansas sued on behalf of all Arkansas clerks in *AYME BROWN, individually and in her official capacity as circuit clerk of Hot Spring County, Arkansas, and on behalf of all circuit clerks in the State of Arkansas v. MERS*. The court dismissed the suit stating that there is no obligation to record assignments in the public records.

Florida, *Jim Fuller, Clerk of the Circuit Court of Duval County, Florida V. MERS Duval County Clerk V. MERS*. June 2012. In this case, the Clerk of Court for Duval County initiated a class action suit in the name of all 67 county Clerk of Courts in Florida. Besides the argument about MERS claiming to be "mortgagee", the Clerk accuses MERS of unlawfully substituting itself for the public records, thereby depriving the clerks of millions of dollars of fees. The court first rejects the plaintiffs standing by stating that while Florida Statute 28.222 authorizes the clerk of courts to record mortgages and related documents, the statute does not provide for a remedy in the case of violation of the statute. The court then discusses each of the counts, such as civil conspiracy and unjust enrichment to show that they lack merit. The discussion that is relevant here concerns MERS usurping the clerk's power to record. The court points out that there is no requirement to record an assignment, nor is a fee required when an assignment is not recorded, nor is MERS' actions prohibited by law. Therefore, p. 19 "… MERS is not usurping any governmental authority or power"

Illinois. In *UNION COUNTY, ILLINOIS; PEOPLE OF THE STATE OF ILLINOIS ex rel; TYLER EDMONDS State's Attorney for the County of Union; and BOBBY TOLER Clerk of the County of Union and on behalf of the County of Union, Illinois and all Counties in Illinois, Plaintiffs, vs. MERSCORP, INC.,* the Judge ruled that there is no obligation to record assignments of mortgage. While the law states that assignments "shall" be recorded in the respective county, the word "shall" relates to how the assignment is recorded (i.e. in the correct county) and not whether the assignment has to be recorded in the first place.

Iowa. *Plymouth County, Iowa v. Merscorp. Et al.* August 2012. As in Kentucky and Florida, the court based its decision on the fact the there is no statutory requirement to record assignments of mortgage. As such, all of the various counts melt away.

Kentucky *CHRISTIAN COUNTY CLERK, by and through its County Clerk, MICHAEL KEM; et. al.* Feb. 21, 2012. U.S. District Court threw out an attempt by various county clerks to claim damages from MERS since they were deprived of recording fees due to the MERS system. The court answered that the law never guaranteed the clerks these revenues. The law was not passed to protect the county clerks but to protect landowners. Failure to record an assignment does not invalidate the sale of the mortgage; the danger involved is the loss of priority. But that is the option of the new owner of the note. Finally, the law did not provide for a remedy for the county clerks. The clerks lacked standing and their complaint was dismissed.

Missouri. The court in *JACKSON COUNTY, MISSOURI, by and through W. STEPHEN NIXON, JACKSON COUNTY COUNSELOR, Plaintiff, vs. MERSCORP, INC.,* dismissed the case stating:"… but no duty to record assignment of deeds of trust exist under Missouri law."

North Carolina. The count clerk of Guilford County, N.C. has filed a very broad attack on the entire mortgage industry. In *Guilford County et al v. LPS et al* the clerk reviews securitization, MERS, robo-signing and other issues. When the clerk rails against MERS for making the chain of title of property unreliable, he is overreaching since MERS is not concerned with actual property. But he correctly criticizes the un-provability of MERS' satisfactions, and the uncertainty revolving around the thousands of "certified" officers of MERS. In this case too, the court decided that there is no obligation to record assignments in the public records.

Minnesota. In August 2013, the United States Court for the District of Minnesota dismissed a lawsuit brought by the Clerks of Court for Ramsey and Hennepin Counties.

Rhode Island. In June of 2013, the court dismissed an action brought by Town of Johnston stating: "The Town's claim fail, however, because Rhode Island law does not require that all mortgages and mortgage assignments be recorded. Absent a statutory requirement to record, there are no damages and therefore, there is no cause of action." (p.1).

In addition, a man named Barrett Bates has taken it upon himself to defend the Clerks of Court in various jurisdictions by suing

MERS. He has sued in 1) Nevada, 2) California, 3) Indiana, 4) Hawaii, 5) Tennessee and 6) Washington DC. Mr. Bates doesn't seem to be getting very far in his endeavors. There are other actions by private persons that attempt to recover moneys from MERS that they claim should have gone to the various clerks of court. Till now, those actions fail for lack of standing. (See the **Texas** case *Huml v. MERS.*)

In summary, the clerks of courts have not gotten very far against MERS. In 2012, and as of mid-2013, all suits against MERS brought by the various clerks of court have failed on the grounds that there is no requirement to record assignments, and nothing prohibits MERS' recordings. While I agree with the courts' decisions, I think it is critical to point out the economic reason that clerks of court are failing against MERS.

Public records were invented three centuries before the Internet. The American economy, with its reliance on real estate financing, would never have thrived without a public system of land records. There are two critical reasons for recording mortgage documents. 1) "Notice" is critical in order to establish priority, and so that prior mortgages can be paid off during conveyance of property. 2) Communication of the lender's address. A loan can be paid off only by correspondence with the servicer of the note. MERS fulfills both functions. 1) MERS mortgages give notice to the public of a lien on property. 2) The MERS' Internet site, and toll-free number, give the public instant information as to the servicer and its address. As long as the public has notice of liens on the property, together with real-time access to the servicer, the essential functions of public recording are fulfilled. The fact that the Holder's address is no longer in the public records is not a barrier to the efficient working of the real estate market. Not only is the average American not injured by the MERS system, there is added value in having real time information about the servicing of mortgages.

SUMMARY #1 - THREE FOCII OF MERS LITIGATION

The three areas of MERS litigation can be sorted as follows:

	Results	Reasoning
MERS and assignments	All states recognize that MERS can assign title to the mortgage back to the latest Holder of the note and execute a satisfaction of mortgage	MERS mortgages declare that MERS is 1) mortgagee but 2) only holds legal title to the mortgage. (i.e. MERS is mortgagee-in-title) Some states also point out that MERS, as nominee, can assign (such as Mass.); but, in my opinion, this is secondary.
MERS as plaintiff as nominee of the lender (Until July 22, 2011)	Most states recognize that MERS could be plaintiff, as nominee for the lender, in a foreclosure action or in a request for relief from stay. New York, Maine and Vermont did not. (But agreed that MERS could foreclose as Holder of the note.)	MERS mortgages declare that 1) MERS is nominee for the lender 2) with the right to foreclose. Minnesota legislation bases this right solely on MERS holding title to the mortgage; no other state agrees.
MERS vs. Clerks of Court	No Clerk of Court has won a suit against MERS.	Court's reasoning: Statutes don't require public recording of assignments; so clerks are not losing anything. My reason: As long as the public has notice of liens in public record, and as long as information regarding the concurrent lender is readily available from MERS, MERS will be allowed to continue to operate its business model.

SUMMARY #2: To What Degree Do The 50 States Accept the MERS Model?

States which accepted the MERS model:			
MERS can 1) Assign and Release Mortgages, and (or) 2) until July 22, 2011, be Plaintiff in a Foreclosure Action as Nominee for the Lender	Alabama Connecticut Idaho Maryland Minnesota Nevada North Dakota Oregon Texas Washington Wyoming	Arizona Florida Illinois Massachusetts Missouri New Hampshire Ohio Pennsylvania Utah West Virginia	California Georgia Kentucky Michigan Montana New Jersey Oklahoma Rhode Island Virginia Wisconsin
States which did not accept the MERS model in whole:			
MERS cannot be Plaintiff in a Foreclose Action as Nominee for the Lender (but can foreclose as Holder) Not relevant after July 22, 2011	MAINE NEW YORK VERMONT		
MERS can act upon the instructions of the lender BUT MERS is not a necessary party	ARKANSAS KANSAS HAWAII INDIANA		
States which didn't join the fray:			
No case addresses the substantive issue of MERS acting as a Plaintiff in a Foreclosure action	Alaska Iowa Nebraska South Carolina	Colorado Louisiana New Mexico South Dakota	Delaware Mississippi North Carolina Tennessee

The Final Word: The Good, The Bad, and The Possible

Out of intense complexities, intense simplicities emerge.

Winston Churchill

MERS was formed to solve a nagging and pervasive problem arising out of the modernization of the real estate market. Notes, which are bearer instruments, can be negotiated in seconds; yet recording the assignment of mortgage for the properties which secure those notes can take days, weeks or even months. MERS solved this problem with an ingenious idea. MERS would hold title to the mortgages of its members. Once an assignment into MERS was recorded in the public record, assignments did not have to be recorded even if the note that it secured was traded a hundred times. Public awareness of the existence of the lien was maintained despite the transfer of ownership of the underlying debt.

This brilliant idea was executed in the most obtuse fashion possible. MERS' documents are poorly drafted. Words with centuries of history are misused. Definitions are mangled. Execution of the MERS business model is beyond irresponsible. It's as if the people at MERS asked themselves: How can we mangle a brilliant idea in the most absurd manner possible? How can we eliminate transparency and accountability? How can we generate litigation in all fifty states, in both state court and federal court? The legal profession added many more layers of confusion by analyzing MERS from a legal point of view, even though MERS is a problem in Title before it is a problem in law.

This lack of clarity generated a general feeling, in the blogosphere, that MERS was some type of evil conspiracy; an undesirable amalgam of the worst of Darth Vader, Lord Voldemort and Sauron, Lord of the Rings. However, once MERS is analyzed from a Title perspective, then the pieces fall into place. Once the components of MERS, notes and mortgages are clearly defined, and the inter-relationships clearly delineated, then the confusion falls away. The legal model was legitimate; MERS went wrong with its obtuse business module.

Cleaning up MERS is not only possible, it is relatively easy. All involved have to clearly understand the definitions for the various terms, and use them correctly. Documents need to be drafted clearly and correctly. "Certified Officers" need to be identified by a MERS' database and by their real employer. MERS must stop its members from issuing Satisfactions of Mortgage in its name.

The confusion about MERS generated confusion in other areas. For instance, in many cases involving MERS, confusion arises as to who Holds the note. This confusion arises from a different anachronism in the real estate market, namely the existence of bearer notes. Paper as a store of value played a critical role in the emergence of the modern economy; but it is no longer needed. Bearer instruments are fading away as paper is replaced by digital currency. The note should be endorsed to payee. An even better solution is to abolish the paper note altogether.

Another issue which often arises in MERS litigation is who to hold responsible for defective foreclosures. The courts should penalize the lending institutions for defective foreclosure, while protecting the buyers of those foreclosure properties. MERS is not the culprit, or even a player here.

In sum, by analyzing MERS, and MERS litigation, from a title perspective, by cleaning up the MERS' operations, and by abolishing bearer notes and foreclosure reversal, we can restore transparency and accountability to real estate conveyance in America.

APPENDIX A:

States that Accepted the MERS Model for Mortgage Assignments and Foreclose Actions (till 7.22.2011)

Disclaimer: This is a title review, not a legal review. I searched for the major cases that either established precedent in the respective state and/or served as landmarks for discussion in courts around the country. Once a state made up its mind as to MERS, there was no need to review the multiple subsequent cases which re-affirmed. If you need to know the latest cases, you need to research that state yourself. The complete texts of the cases reviewed below are available online at www.mersnews.com

Citations are available in Appendix C.

ALABAMA

Crum v. LaSalle Bank, N.A. (2009) deals with MERS and assignments. This is an important case in that it was cited all over the country. While the court made a correct determination, it muddied the waters in its analysis.

The borrower challenged the validity of the foreclosure by attacking the assignment of mortgage that MERS made to the final Holder of the note, La Salle Bank, N.A. The borrower claimed that since MERS did not have an ownership interest in the debt, MERS could not convey the right to foreclose. The court correctly answers this contention by stating that the borrower executed the mortgage document which states that MERS has the right to foreclose, and p.4 "...MERS assigned to the assignee all the rights formerly held by it and by the lender." This concluding sentence of the case is correct but is very different than the analysis in the body of the case.

The mortgage document reads that MERS holds "legal title to the interest granted by Borrower in this Security Instrument" and that MERS "..has the right: to exercise any or all of those interests…..". Those interests concern the pledge of the land as security. The court quotes these passages and concludes that MERS holds the lender's interests "..in the mortgaged property including selling the note and the mortgage to a third party". Not so. MERS can never sell a note since MERS never owns the note and MERS is never empowered to sell the note. What actually happened is that the original lender sold the note, and MERS simply assigned title to the mortgage to the new owner of the note. (In this Appeal, the borrower tried to challenge the negotiation of the note but the court refused to hear arguments that had not been asserted at trial).

To be fair to the court, it is clear that the court was misled by the incorrectly drafted assignment of mortgage. The assignment reads that the mortgage is assigned as well as "…all moneys now owing or that may hereafter become due or owing in respect thereof…". This is similar to the thousands - or millions - of incorrectly worded assignments which purport to convey the note as well as the mortgage. As we have stated throughout this manual, MERS cannot assign the note since MERS never owns the note, nor is it empowered to assign the note. An identical absurdity caused havoc in the Missouri case *Bellistri* (see below). In summary, the court correctly determined that the assignment of mortgage, and the foreclosure, were valid. But the court's reasoning was not clearly thought out.

In a late case (2010), *Debra A. Henderson v. Merscorp, Inc. et al*, the Circuit Court of Montgomery County declared that MERS has standing to foreclose. This was affirmed by the Alabama Supreme Court in Sept. 2011, when the issue was moot. (MERS stopped the practice of foreclosing in its name on July 22, 2011.)

ARIZONA

Arizona, like the other states in the Ninth District (California, Arizona, Idaho, Oregon, Washington, Montana and Nevada), has no problem with MERS. An oft cited case from 2009 is *Cervantes v. Countrywide Home Loans, Inc.* in which the borrower challenges the legitimacy of MERS by claiming the MERS is not the real beneficiary. The U.S. District Court of Arizona found that:

1)   The fact that MERS does not have all the rights of the beneficiary (such as the right to collect mortgage payments) does not mean that MERS' status as beneficiary is a sham.

2)   The fact that the note was sold without public recording is irrelevant; that, after all, is the basis of the MERS system.

3)   MERS may act as the "beneficiary" of the deed-of-trust and appoint a successor trustee.

In *Ciardi v. Lending Company, Inc.* (2010) the same court again rejected all of the borrower's attacks on MERS' authority and standing.

1)   The court declares emphatically the MERS is the beneficiary as designated by the deed-of-trust which the borrowers "freely entered into". That deed-of-trust authorizes MERS to "take any action to enforce the loan, including the right to foreclose..."

2)   More importantly, the court declares that MERS, as beneficiary, does not have to prove that it has an interest in the actual note.

(Court is basically stating that MERS is the beneficiary-in-title, but not the beneficiary-in-equity).

3) Assignments of deed-of-trust do not have to be recorded to be valid.

4) Finally, borrower's contention that the sale of the note some-how disconnects MERS from the note-holder is disproved by the agency language of the deed-of-trust which includes "and its assigns."

CALIFORNIA

In a string of cases in 2011, California consistently ruled that the MERS model is valid. In *Jose Gomes v. Countrywide Home Loans, Inc.* the borrower challenged the authority of MERS to initiate a foreclo-sure action, stating that MERS was not the owner, nor was it acting on authority of the owner. The court rejected this outright by simply reciting California Statute 2924 (a) (1) in that foreclosure may be initi-ated by a "trustee, mortgagee, or beneficiary, or any of their autho-rized agents". Furthermore, there is no requirement for the initiator of a foreclosure to prove his authority in a court of law. That would defeat the whole justification for a non-judicial system. The whole point of the Title-Theory system is that non-judicial foreclosure is easier and cheaper. Having to prove authority to foreclosure would defeat the whole purpose. What is important for our purposes is not the court's refusal to allow a judicial step to be introduced into non-judicial foreclosure; but rather the recognition that p. 11 footnote: "… under California law MERS may initiate a foreclosure as the nominee, or agent of the noteholder."

An interesting argument revolves around who is the beneficiary. The borrower argues that MERS is not the beneficiary of the deed-of-trust, as that term has been understood for generations – regardless of what is written in the borrower's deed-of-trust. The other side argued that MERS is nominee of the beneficiary since it is the agent of the lender. The court felt that it was not necessary to decide this issue since MERS could clearly initiate foreclosure as agent for the Holder. This is a fascinating argument because it parallels the endless arguments in Lien-Theory States as to whether or not MERS is the mortgagee. One side will argue that MERS can't be the mortgagee since that is not how the term has been used for the last few centuries. And the other side will argue that state statute, and/or the mortgage itself, allows MERS to be mortgagee. Both of these conflicts are resolved by the terms I developed in "MERS, Notes and Mortgages". In Lien-Theory States, if we label MERS as the mortgagee-in-title, and the lender as the mortgagee-in-equity, then the conflict melts away. The same here. If we label MERS as the beneficiary-in-title, and the lender as the beneficiary-in-equity, then the issue is resolved.

Fontenot v. Wells Fargo Bank, N.A. deals with the relationship between MERS and the note. The borrower claimed that MERS has to prove that note was assigned. The court rejects this as extraneous to the non-judicial process. Secondly, the borrower claims that MERS cannot assign the note since it has no interest in it. The Court rejects this claim too, stating that while MERS cannot assign in its own right, it can assign the note as agent. I believe that the court overreached. MERS cannot assign the note because MERS is never the Holder of the note; and MERS cannot assign the note as agent because the power to assign is not delegated to MERS.

But the court redeems itself by stating that the real issue is whether the plaintiff was assigned the note from some entity – and not whether that entity happened to be MERS. This is the correct solution to *Bellistri* from Missouri. There the court stated that MERS cannot assign the note, therefore the plaintiff doesn't hold the note. But that is the wrong conclusion. The plaintiff could have (and actually did) obtain the note from the original lender. This solution was also offered in the important New Jersey case *MERS v. Raftogianis* and in Massachusetts *In re Lopez*.

Robinson v. OneWest This case has the same situation as *Ferguson* and affirms that case. But more important is the court's development of the idea, stated in *Fontenot,* that the public record is not the only proof of authority; i.e. the public records is not the only medium to prove standing. While the deed-in-trust is recorded and establishes a chain of authority, there are other documents which convey authority and which are not recorded in the public record, specifically the note and the creation of agency. An unrecorded document can assign the power to foreclose and can be ratified retroactively. In addition, the note can be assigned in an unrecorded document. This mechanism is not well understood by laymen, lawyers, or judges. While mortgages and deeds-in-trust have to be recorded to establish the chain of title of the security interest, the underlying asset – the actual debt - is not recorded in the public records. Furthermore, there usually is a time gap between the assignment of the note, and the parallel recording of the security interest. The judge in this case understood this dynamic, which is more than can be said for the Missouri Court in *Bellistri.*

Finally, *Calvo vs. HSBC* is worth reading because of a very interesting discussion on the differences between mortgages and deed-of-trust, both of which are available in California, even though California basically adheres to Title-Theory and most real estate is transacted through deeds-of-trust. The court explains that the difference was determined back in 1908, in *Stockwell v. Barnum.* In that case, the court decided that assignments of the deed-of-trust had to be recorded prior to sale in order to prove authority to foreclose. However, an assignment of the beneficial interest of a deed-of-trust does not have to be recorded since p. **5 "…the lenders had no power of sale, and only the trustee could transfer title, it was immaterial who held the note."** They cite *Stockwell* at p. 416: "The transferee of a negotiable promissory note, payment of which is secured by a deed-of-trust whereby the title to the property and power of sale in case of default invested in a third party as trustee, is not an encumbrancer to whom power of sale is given, within the meaning of section 858." They could also have cited *Jackson* from Minnesota.

CONNECTICUT

MERS v. Ventura et al. No problems here: "MERS is a separate corporation that is acting solely as a nominee for Lender and Lender's successors and assigns. Thus, there is no question that the named plaintiff is the correct party to bring this action".

FLORIDA

While Florida's courts accepted the MERS model, they repeatedly did so for the wrong reason. The courts kept trying to tie MERS to the note, which is incorrect. The power of foreclosure rests in the mortgage, not in the note. Several important Florida cases are discussed in Section 15 of "MERS, Notes, and Mortgages".

GEORGIA

Georgia was the last state to weigh in on MERS. When I first posted cases from around the country on my website, www.mersnews.com Georgia did not seem to have any major cases. In 2011 though, courts in Georgia decided several cases in favor of MERS. While Georgia is a Title-Theory state, it differs from most in that the deed-of-trust does not establish a trustee to hold title. The lender holds title directly, pending payment of the loan.

In *James L. Drake, Jr., Trustee v. Citizens Bank of Effingham etal*, the court decided that MERS could hold title to the deed-of-trust. While most states call the beneficiary of the deed-of-trust the "beneficiary", in Georgia that party is called the "grantee". The court found nothing wrong with MERS assigning the deed-of-trust back to the lender. This is the equivalent of an assignment of mortgage in a Lien-Theory state.

While I could find no case in which MERS was the actual plaintiff in a foreclosure, many of the cases that dealt with the validity of MERS' assignments stated very clearly that the deed-of-trust grants MERS the right to invoke the power of sale as nominee of the lender.

IDAHO

An early case that was cited as the "end of MERS" was *In Re Darrell Royce Sheridan, Sherry Ann Sheridan* in U.S. Bankruptcy Court in Idaho. In this case, MERS, as nominee of the lender, moved for relief from stay. In this case, the court denied MERS' motion because the cited lender could not prove that it held the note. P. 15: "Thus, even if a 'nominee' such as MERS could properly bring a motion for stay relief in the name of and on behalf of the real party in interest – the entity that has rights in and pecuniary interest under the Note secured by the Deed-of-trust – nothing of record adequately establishes who that entity actually is." What we have here is a case of factual confusion, and not a conclusion of law. Yet this case was widely cited for different interpretations of this sentence. What did the court mean by "even if"? I would think that the court is implying that MERS cannot bring a motion; if the court did think that MERS could bring such a motion, it would have written:" Even though MERS could properly

132

bring a motion for stay of relief on behalf of the real property of interest…" But the court chose "even if" not "even though". In any case,
this discussion is speculative since *Sheridan* did not come down on
one side or the other. Both *Sheridan* and *In re Laverl H. Wilhelm* from
Idaho are excellent discussions of standing and the right to enforce
the note.

In re Sheridan (2009) was often cited as ammunition against MERS. But
that case did not decide anything about MERS. The court felt that it
could not determine who held the note. It did not decide whether or
not MERS could bring a motion for Relief from Stay.

As cases percolated across the state, most districts did not have trou-
ble with the process of MERS assigning its interest. For instance, in
Stanton vs. First Horizon, the Fourth Judicial District Court found that
MERS could assign the deed-of-trust. So does the First Judicial District
Court in *Bryan vs. GMAC*.

In any case, the Supreme Court of Idaho took up this issue and had
no problem with MERS assigning the deed-of-trust. In *Trotter v. Bank
of New York Mellon*, the court states, backhandedly, that cases cited
by the plaintiff do not support plaintiff's p. 7: "…assertion that under
Idaho law, MERS could not assign its interest in the deed-of-trust."
The court went further and states that plaintiff can't show from the
deed-of-trust that MERS is not the beneficiary. The results are clear
cut; though it would have been clearer if the court had used the terms
developed in "MERS, Notes, and Mortgages".

ILLINOIS

In *MERS v. Jessie Barnes*, the court correctly determined that MERS can
be the plaintiff in a foreclosure action. The court points out that as
nominee for the lender, and as holder of title to the mortgage, and

having the power to foreclose, (all of which the borrower agreed to in the mortgage instrument) MERS has the power to initiate a foreclosure action.

KENTUCKY

Deutsche Bank v. Moody. MERS assigned the mortgage back to lender after complaint was filed. Court found nothing wrong with this.

MARYLAND

Maryland accepts the judicial determinations of the majority of other states, namely that MERS can assign the mortgage. I did not find anything especially original or different in Maryland's cases. This quote from *Suss v. JP Morgan Chase Bank, N.A.* seems to sum it up: p. 11 "...courts that have considered the issue have found that the system of recordation is proper and assignments made through that system are valid".

Massachusetts

An early and oft cited case is *In re Huggins* (2006) in which MERS hits a double. The court gets directly to the point: MERS is the nominee p. 4 "...understood as a person designated to act in place of another". And since the mortgage document itself grants the power of sale to MERS, therefore MERS can foreclose on behalf of the lender. The court sees no problem with this and engages in no further discussion about being a plaintiff in a foreclosure action. Then the court discusses the right to seek relief from stay. The criteria in Massachusetts for this power is "... a colorable claim to the Property". Again, the court holds, without any discussion, that since MERS has the right as p. 5 "nominee mortgagee" to foreclose, it therefore has the right to seek relief from stay.

The term "nominee mortgagee" is an interesting joinder of the two key terms. Usually, being an agent for the lender is enough to prove standing in a foreclosure case. It is interesting to speculate why the court needed to add "mortgagee". Possibly, the extra modifier added enough bearing to MERS that the decision becomes unassailable.

In discussing cases from New York, the court issues the following gem: p. 5 "…the logic of a denial of MERS's foreclosure right as a mortgagee would lead to anomalous and perhaps inequitable results, to wit, if MERS cannot foreclose though named as mortgagee, then either [the lender] can foreclose though not named as mortgagee or no one can foreclose, outcomes not reasonably or demonstrably intended by the parties".

In Re: Lopez (2009) is another widely cited Massachusetts case. While the case is a request for relief from stay by the Holder of the note, MERS comes up because of its assignment of mortgage. The defendant claimed that an assignment of the mortgage, without the note, is a nullity. The court disagreed by citing a case from 1948, Boruchoff v. Ayvasian 323 Mass. 1, 10, 79 N.E. 2d 892: "…where a mortgage and the obligation secured thereby are held by different persons, the mortgage is regarded as an incident to the obligation, and therefore, held in trust for the benefit of the owner of the obligation". And then the Court holds: p. 9 "…even though MERS never had possession of the Note, it was legally holding the Mortgage in trust for the Note holder". This is in accordance with Minnesota's Jackson: that the mortgagee-in-title has a trust relationship with the mortgagee-in-equity. This court's decision rests on MERS being mortgagee-in-title. The court goes further and holds that MERS also has assignment power as nominee of the lender. Most courts don't require agency power when it comes to assignment. But this court felt that agency reinforces ownership in this case.

It is worthwhile to note that the court correctly analyzed MERS' interest in the property and declared that MERS never Held the note. And the court sees no harm in the fact that the assignment of mortgage includes verbiage assigning the note, even though MERS cannot assign the note; it can only assign the mortgage. This is diametrically different than Missouri in *Bellistri* which took MERS to task for purporting to assign a note.

By 2011 Massachusetts had clearly determined that MERS can assign the mortgage, foreclose on the mortgage, and request relief from stay. *In re Marron* reviews all of these and sums up all of that state's main cases on MERS. The case starts off declaring that MERS holds title to the mortgage. Then goes a step further, as in *In Re Lopez,* and declares that the holder of the mortgage does so as trustee for the Holder of the note, with fiduciary duty to the Holder of the note. The court declares that one of those duties is the right to assign the mortgage. The court correctly checks the MERS Membership Agreement and cites Rule 8 which instructs MERS to assign the mortgage when such request is made by the note Holder.

MICHIGAN

A controversial judgment issued by the Court of Appeals created much drama in Michigan which had to be settled by Michigan's Supreme Court. These cases are interesting because they go to the heart of the ownership model developed in this treatise.

Michigan allows both judicial and non-judicial foreclosure. Most courts seemed to agree that MERS can assign its interest, and can foreclose in a judicial setting. But in *Residential Funding Co. LLC v. Saurman,* The Court of Appeals decided that MERS could not foreclose by advertisement (a non-judicial process). The debate centered on the following sub-paragraph in Michigan's law concerning foreclosure by advertisement:

MCL 600.3204 (1) (d) *The party foreclosing the mortgage is either the owner of the indebtedness or of an interest in the indebtedness secured by the mortgage or the servicing agent of the mortgage.*

This condition for foreclosure seems to bar MERS since the foreclosing party must either be an owner of the note ("the indebtedness"), or an owner of part of the note, or a servicing agent. MERS is never the owner of the note or of part of the note, and never acts as servicing agent for the mortgage. The court correctly rejected an attempt by counsel to claim that the MERS Membership Agreement gave MERS an interest in the note. (To the contrary; as discussed repeatedly above, MERS is never the owner and the Membership Agreement prescribes fines for even claiming as much). And the court declared that the foreclosure in this case was "void *ab initio*". So while the court does not object to MERS assigning its interest, or to MERS foreclosing in a judicial process, the court (with one judge dissenting) forbade MERS from foreclosing by advertisement.

In any case, *Residential Funding* set off a storm of cases testing the waters. While many appeals to reverse foreclosure were dismissed because the redemption period had run out, other borrowers were able to have their cases dismissed based on *Residential Funding.* The Michigan Supreme Court realized that the validity of thousands of foreclosures was in doubt. In Aug. 2011 the Court stayed proceedings in a different case – *PB REIT, INC. v. Debabneh*, and allowed appeals in that case and for *Residential Funding.* In Nov. 2011, the Michigan Supreme Court reversed the ruling of *Residential Funding* with a two page decision. It gave two reasons:

1) First, the court accepted the dissenting judge's logic that MERS is "the owner ...of an interest" of the note since it owns part of the interest securing that note.

2) The second reason given by the court stands on much firmer grounds. In explaining MCL 600.3204 (1) (d) (previous page) P.2: "We discern no indication that ... the Legislature...meant to establish a new legal framework in which an undisputed record holder of a mortgage, such as MERS, no longer possesses the statutory authority to foreclose". Michigan had always allowed the record holder of the mortgage to foreclose (Michigan is a Title-Theory state), and the emergence of MERS didn't change anything.

MINNESTOA

Minnesota allows foreclosure by advertisement which is a non-judicial method. The main Minnesota case, *Jackson v. MERS,* was discussed at length in Chapter 11 of the Tutorial because of its clear understanding of the components of notes and mortgages. It correctly showed that title to the security instrument can be held by a party other than the owner of the equity in the security instrument (who by force is the owner of the note). The court held that MERS can hold title to the mortgage while the lender holds the equitable interest.

The Court points out that in 2004, the Minnesota legislature passed an amendment (now known as the "MERS Statute") to the recording act, by which the nominee of the mortgagee can foreclose in its own right, as long as the power to do so is recorded in the public record: p.9 "....the holder of legal title to a mortgage can exercise the mortgage's power of sale if that title appears of record". So MERS can foreclose solely on the basis of its holding title to the mortgage. But that theory holds only in Minnesota.

MISSOURI

One of the most important cases in the unfolding history of MERS is the Bellistri Appeal's case, and its subsequent overturn in Federal Court. This case is discussed in the section "States That Hold that MERS is Not a Necessary Party" in the Title Analysis of MERS Litigation above. The importance of this case rests on the Federal Court determining that MERS is a party of interest, and its right to notice is guaranteed by the Fourteenth Amendment of the Constitution. This should be the answer to the courts in states such as Hawaii, Kansas, Indiana and Arkansas that held that MERS is not an indispensable party.

MONTANA

Like other Title-Theory states, Montana does not require the Trustee to prove he/she has the original note. There is no "show me the note" requirement. In *Waide v. US Bank National Association*, the court pointed out that the Small Tract Financing Act allows the beneficiary to appoint a successor trustee, which was what happened in this case.

NEVADA

Nevada cases are discussed above in the Chapter V.2.a. State Jurisdiction vs. Federal Jurisdiction. In this state, it was the state courts that got it right; the Federal court got it wrong.

NEW HAMPSHIRE

In *Powers v. Aurora Loan Services*, the New Hampshire Superior Court was very firm in determining that MERS has authority to assign the mortgage, based on agency. (p. 10 In New Hampshire the assignment of mortgage does not have to be recorded!)

NEW JERSEY

MERS v. Raftogianis. This is a must-read case for its explanation of notes and mortgages. And while the court had no problems with the MERS model, the court invalidated a foreclosure because the plaintiff could not prove possession as of the date of the complaint. An original mortgage was executed in 2004. MERS executed an assignment of mortgage in 2009 but there was no proof that plaintiff had the note yet.

On a different matter, the court found no problem with the fact the standard MERS' assignment is drafted incorrectly. P. 27: "It was entirely appropriate to argue that the February 2009 assignment from MERS, as nominee for American Home Acceptance, to the Bank of New York as Trustee, was ineffective. From the court's perspective, that assignment was, at best, a distraction. The actual transfers of interests in the note and mortgage occurred in different ways. There was no reason, however, that plaintiff could not acquire the right to enforce the note and mortgage through those other transactions." This contrasts with the Missouri Appeals court in *Bellistri*. The fact that the assignment of mortgage purports to assign the note, and really doesn't, does not invalidate the assignment of mortgage.

NORTH DAKOTA

Please see Chapter V.2.b. "Can MERS Ever be Holder of the Note".

OHIO

In MERS v. Mosley the borrower raises the standard argument that MERS, having no interest in the property, has no standing to foreclose. The court argues that the power to foreclose has two sources: 1) It is given by the lender to MERS in the foreclosure document; p. 13 "MERS …has had a contractual right to foreclose on the Mortgage." 2) MERS can foreclose as nominee of the lender. The agency power overrides the fact that MERS has no interest in the property.

OREGON

Oregon was initially considered to be an anti-MERS state but that changed. The national press had latched on to two early cases which, in the end, did not carry much weight.

The drama started with a decision from the U.S. District Court for Oregon. In *Natche D.Rinegard-Guirma v. Bank of America*, (2010) a Federal judge stopped a foreclosure, not on the merits, but because of the lack of guidance from state courts concerning MERS. P. 9 "Absent a decision from the Oregon Supreme Court or the Oregon Court of Appeals, and absent further briefing from the parties on this specific issue, I am at least initially persuaded that Rinegard-Guirma has a likelihood of success on the merits." This was seized upon as a defeat for MERS. This case even made it into the New York Times (Oct. 18, 2010). But anyone reading the case could see that the judge didn't really decide anything. He correctly felt that the proper forum for deciding real estate law was the state court system and not the federal court system. This case was not a defeat for MERS but simply a vote to abstain.

Another ostensibly anti-MERS case that garnered national attention was *Hooker v. Trustee Services* (2011). Yet this case actually didn't decide anything. The judge decided not to establish precedent but to p. 16 "…resolve the controversy on narrow grounds." Since the plaintiff filed the notice of default four days before MERS assigned it the mortgage, the judge rules that the plaintiff had no authority to foreclose. This is hardly a defeat for MERS; it simply demanded strict adherence to procedural rules. Yet the national press seized on this as a great defeat for MERS.

Actually, two months earlier, in March 2011, another Federal Court judge issued a strong decision upholding MERS as beneficiary of the deed-of-trust. In *Shelton R. Bertrand et al v. Suntrust Mortgage, Inc.*, the court declared unequivocally that MERS can assign the deed-of-trust, and act as beneficiary to initiate foreclosure. This was in accordance with every other state of the Ninth Circuit.

Likewise, many Circuit Courts for the various counties of Oregon have issued decisions validating MERS as beneficiary. An early precedent was set by the County of Josephine *in David M. Buckland v. Aurora Loan Services*. The court agreed that:

1) MERS can be the beneficiary of the Deed-of-Trust.
2) MERS can assign its rights as beneficiary.
3) MERS can substitute the Trustee of the deed-of-trust.
4) MERS can initiate the foreclosure.

The court also re-iterated what courts in every other state in the Ninth District knows: that to initiate non-judicial foreclosure, it is not necessary for the initiator to have the note. In summary, despite hopes by the anti-MERS crusaders that Oregon would join Vermont and Maine in invalidating MERS, Oregon came round to the rest of the Ninth District in accepting MERS' power to act as beneficiary (in a Title Theory state), to assign the deed-of-trust, and to initiate foreclosure.

OKLAHOMA

MERS, Inc. v. William C. Warden, et al., unpublished. Press reports that court allowed MERS to be plaintiff in this foreclosure action.

PENNSYLVANIA

In *MERS v. Ralich*, MERS filed for foreclosure as nominee for lender, and actually completed the sale in its name. The borrowers claimed that MERS lacked authority to make the sale (not stating why). The court simply cited the mortgage which "vests MERS with the authority, as nominee, to enforce the loan."

RHODE ISLAND

(Note: Rhode Island was a Lien-Theory state but now allows non-judicial foreclosure when the mortgage includes statutory language for power of sale).

Rhode Island, in *Bucci v. Lehman Brothers* follows Massachusetts, citing the language and logic used in *Huggins*. The borrower claimed that MERS lacks standing to foreclose since the Statutory Power of Sale is given to the lender. The court quotes the paragraph of the mortgage in which MERS is appointed nominee for Lender and Lender's assigns and granted the Statutory Power of Sale to MERS. The court also quotes the mortgage in which MERS is named as mortgagee. P. 11 "Here, the Court finds that MERS is the mortgagee because the Mortgage execute by the Buccis so states."

I find it interesting that the borrower would try to disprove MERS' authority by calling it a "nominee-mortgagee". Since either term – nominee or mortgagee - could be used to prove MERS' authority, combining them certainly wouldn't work for the borrower. In any case, the correct doctrine for asserting MERS' authority is agency – namely that it is the nominee. Claiming that MERS is the mortgagee might not be sufficient since, as we explained in "MERS, Notes, and Mortgages", MERS is the mortgagee-in-title and does not have all the rights that abide in the security interest. The judge's declaration that MERS is the mortgagee needs to be modified to "mortgagee-in-title".

Another interesting aspect of this case is the following assertion by the judge as to MERS' power to foreclose: p. 7 "As a matter of fact, it could be argued that if the Lender sought to foreclose it would be challenged as a stranger to the title." This is an excellent rebuttal to the Kansas court in *Kessler* which argued that MERS is not a necessary party.

TEXAS

In *Athey v. MERS* the court quickly disposed of the borrower's claim that MERS cannot foreclose since it neither Holds nor owns the note by noting that the Deed-of-trust gave MERS the authority to foreclose.

UTAH

For a sparsely populated state, Utah's dockets are chock full of cases concerning MERS. Across the board, Utah accepts the MERS legal model. While Utah allows both judicial and non-judicial foreclosure, the main cases all concern non-judicial foreclosure.

In *Marty v. MERS* the court finds that MERS has authority to foreclose and to appoint a new trustee. The court accepts the MERS model by commenting that a sale of the underlying debt does not affect MERS standing or powers.

The borrower contends that Rule 17 of the Federal Rules of Civil Procedure preclude MERS from having standing in a foreclosure. Rule 17 reads as follows:

17(a)(1) "..an action must be prosecuted in the name of the real party in interest." The borrower claims that MERS is not a real party of interest. The court answers that the problem is solved by the end of Rule 17 which states:

"The following may sue in their own names without joining the person for whose benefit the action is brought........a party with whom or in whose name a contract has been made for another's benefit..". Since MERS clearly is in contract to act for the benefit of the lender, MERS has standing in this non-judicial foreclosure.

In multiple subsequent cases, such as *Wareing v. Meridias Capital*, and *Wade v. Meridias Capital*, the U.S. District Court of Utah, Central Division, repeatedly states the MERS has the authority to act as beneficiary under the Deed-of-trust. The Court also re-iterates that the note has not been split from the mortgage (as explained in "MERS, Notes, and Mortgages"). In *Wade*, the court goes beyond its finding in *Marty* stating that there is no need to discuss MERS' standing since the Trustee has the right to foreclose regardless of who holds the note. P. 6 "Possession and proof of the Note are not a requirement for non-judicial foreclosure."

In *Webb v. CitiMortgage, Inc.,* the Fourth Judicial District Court in and For Utah County repeats the findings of the cases we cited and is very emphatic as to the impossibility of splitting the note: p. 3 "...the Note has not been split from the Trust Deed; in fact, such splitting is legally impossible."

VIRGINIA

Virginia has no problem with MERS model. In *Graves.v MERS* the court finds that MERS can foreclose and that MERS can assign the Deed-of-Trust.

1) The borrower claimed that MERS has no authority since only the lender has certain powers. In reply, the court simply quoted the verbiage of the security instrument which appoints MERS as nominee for the lender with all the powers to foreclose and change trustees.

2) The borrower tried a novel tact in this case by suggesting that the term "if necessary to comply with the law" means that MERS can only change trustees if the law requires it. The court correctly disregards the bad syntax of the clause (it should read "when necessary") and states the security document clearly defines MERS' powers.

3) Borrower also claims that Virginia statute grants the power to appoint a trustee to the holder of at least 50% of the note. The court answers that the statute fills in the void where the contract is silent. Since the Deed-of-trust gives the power to MERS, there is no violation of the statute.

Besides these claims, the borrower tried to use interpretive tools on the security instrument to attack MERS. But the court's theme in this opinion is that the Deed-of-trust is a contract and as such needs to be read as a whole. Virginia contract law must be obeyed. Finally, the borrower and the court get into a "MERS is the Beneficiary" vs. "MERS is not the Beneficiary" argument. The court simply relies on the bare language of the deed. They both would have benefitted from the terms explained in "MERS, Notes, and Mortgages", namely, MERS is not the beneficiary-in-equity, but it is the beneficiary-in-title.

WASHINGTON

Like the other states in the Ninth District, Washington has no problem with the MERS legal model. In *Vawter v. Quality Loan*

Service the borrower challenged MERS' ability to be the beneficiary since MERS does not benefit at all from the loan. The borrower explains that since MERS is only a database of mortgages, MERS cannot possibly play a role as beneficiary. Consequently, MERS' assignment of the Deed-of-trust is invalid. The court simply says – not necessarily. Even if "....MERS exists to maintain records regarding the ownership of mortgages, this does not mean that MERS cannot hold a beneficial interest under the Deed-of-trust." The court doesn't even bother to verbalize the conclusion that there is no reason to invalidate MERS' assignment.

In 2012, the Supreme Court of Washington changed direction in *Kristin Bain v. Metropolitan Mortgage Group et al* stating that MERS is not the beneficiary (!) and therefore cannot appoint a new Trustee for the purposes of foreclosure. But the court then confused everyone by stating that it is unable to determine the legal effect of this pronouncement. What the court giveth, the court taketh away. In any case, if MERS cannot appoint a new trustee, the lender can. So while this decision does call into question the MERS model as discussed in this book, it does not change anything on the ground. For the moment.

WEST VIRGINIA

In *Wittenberg v. First Independent Mortgage* p. 22: "Any representation that MERS has the authority to initiate foreclosure is not false if made prior to assignment...."

WISCONSIN

MERS, Inc. v. Degner – Unpublished. Press reports claim that the court allowed MERS to be plaintiff in this foreclosure action.

WYOMING

In *In Re Martinez*, the borrower claimed that MERS does not have the right to assign the mortgage. The judge answers that as nominee, MERS can "take any action required of the Lender" as per the verbiage of the security instrument, and therefore, has authority to assign the mortgage. I think that when it comes to assignment, the court is better off arguing that MERS holds title to the security instrument and as such *must* be the assignor.

APPENDIX B:

States that Determined that MERS CANNOT be a Plaintiff in Litigation as Nominee for the Lender (but can if it becomes Holder of the note)

Three states never came around to the MERS model of allowing MERS to be plaintiff in a foreclosure action as "nominee" of the lender: Maine, Vermont and New York.

MAINE

One of the standout cases that was trumpeted as the "end of MERS" is *MERS v. Saunders*, issued by the Supreme Court of Maine. This case received attention in the national press because it seemed to put a brake on MERS by declaring that MERS cannot be a plaintiff in a foreclosure action.

The court quotes the standard verbiage found in the subject mortgage assigning to MERS the right to foreclose:

"[Borrowers] understand and agree that MERS holds only legal title to the rights granted by [Borrowers] in this Security Instrument, but, if, necessary to comply with law or custom, MERS (as nominee for Lender and Lender's successors and assigns) has the right: 1) to exercise any or all of those, including, but not limited to, the right to foreclose........"

This is standard verbiage in all MERS mortgages. But the court refuses to accept the validity of that assignment. P.8 "The only rights conveyed to MERS.....are bare legal title to the property for the sole purpose of recording the mortgage…". Namely, the right to foreclose was not successfully transferred by the mortgage document.

The court's reasoning is as follows:

1) According to Maine statute, only "…the mortgagee or any person claiming under the mortgagee may proceed for the purpose of foreclosure by a civil action…"

2) The court then declares that a "fundamental rule of statutory interpretation" is that words must be "give their plain and ordinary meanings". What is the plain and common understanding of "mortgagee"?

3) Citing Black's Law Dictionary, mortgagee is quoted to be "one to whom property is mortgaged" meaning a "mortgage creditor, or lender". The court continues: "In other words, a mortgagee is a party that is entitled to enforce the debt obligation that is secure by a mortgage." And since MERS does not qualify under any of the classes off UCC 3.301, MERS cannot enforce the note.

One could argue that Maine Statute itself gives the power to foreclose not only to the mortgagee, but also to "any person claiming under the mortgagee". Couldn't the mortgagee in title, with an explicit assignment of the right to foreclose, be considered a party "claiming under the mortgagee"? All of the states that acknowledge MERS' right to foreclose do so on the basis of agency; namely the fact that the right to foreclose has been assigned to MERS. And since MERS never acts on its own accord, but only as a literal extension of the lender, is there a need to read Maine Statute so narrowly as to close out MERS' right to foreclose?

Nevertheless, the court concludes that p. 9 "MERS does not qualify as a mortgagee pursuant to our foreclosure statute.. and therefore, the right to foreclose was not assigned". The judges view MERS as nominee in the narrowest terms, and ignore the text of the mortgage instrument, which is a contractual document and binding on all parties. The Maine Supreme Court, like the courts in Vermont and New York decided, that Statute overrides the contract between the parties.

By the way, the note was assigned to the plaintiff bank after MERS filed the complaint. The court could have dismissed the case on this simple defect.

VERMONT

Vermont is another New England state that took a stand against MERS and thereby garnered national attention. The 2009 case *MERS v. Johnston* is a standard foreclosure case. First the judge correctly determines that MERS does not have standing in its own right to bring a foreclosure action. This is consistent with most courts across the country, or all states except for Minnesota; for no other state made a determination that MERS could foreclose based on its being the mortgagee-in-title. This is consistent with the laws of notes and mortgages. The note can only be enforced by the holder or the holder's agent. The holder is the party in possession of the note which is either endorsed to the holder or in blank. Clearly MERS is neither. Then the judge turns to analyzing MERS' powers as nominee of the lender. Here he cites *Huggins* (see above) and takes the Massachusetts' court to task on multiple points:

1) The Vermont Court criticizes *Huggins* for allowing MERS to foreclose based on the language of the mortgage document. "Once again, this conclusion does not take into account

that MERS held only "legal title" and not the note. Therefore, MERS could not enforce the mortgage as record mortgagee". Here, the Vermont Court is simply repeating the first part of its analysis that MERS does not have the right as mortgagee to foreclose. But the point under discussion is whether MERS can foreclose as nominee; and the Vermont Court does not address that issue.

2)   The Vermont Court correctly points out that Massachusetts law empowers the mortgagee with the power of sale. Once again, that is not the issue.

3)   The Vermont Court then simply says that it does not accept "nominee" to mean "agent" and cites the Black's Law definition of "nominee" as a "very limited" agency. But the Court does not explain why that limited scope can't include the power to foreclose. Ignoring the language of the mortgage, the court states "There is no indication that MERS was an agent or power-of-attorney for the lender WMC." Most courts dealing with this issue have explicitly disagreed with this conclusion.

4)   The Vermont Court then interprets the boilerplate term "when necessary to comply with law and custom" as a limitation on MERS' right to foreclose. Most other courts have gotten around that problem by reciting paragraph 22 of the mortgage, which is standard, in which the mortgagee is given the right to foreclose.

5)   Most importantly, the Vermont Court challenges Huggins to explain its view that the note and mortgage are not disconnected. P. 15 "In *Huggins*, there did appear to be a disconnection, as the lender held the Note while MERS held bare legal title. The Court fails to see how MERS's very limited role

as a "nominee" can somehow connect the severed note and mortgage." The Vermont Court missed the point that since MERS held "bare legal title" to the mortgage, the lender continued to hold beneficial title to the mortgage. As such, there was no disconnect between the equity of the note and the equity of the mortgage, which as we have stated countless times, is a unity.

Interestingly, the Vermont Court hits the bull's-eye when it states that all of this could be avoided if MERS would assign the mortgage back to the lender before foreclosure is initiated. MERS finally understood this point and stopped foreclosure in its name as of July 22, 2011. Nevertheless, the court's refusal to allow MERS to foreclose revolves around two arguments. The first is a very narrow reading of the word "nominee", together with a rejection of the plain terms of the mortgage contract. The second argument is the oft-repeated, and mistaken, argument that the note and mortgage have been split. "MERS, Notes, and Mortgages" shows that this argument is a misunderstanding of the mechanics of notes and mortgages.

NEW YORK

New York courts have grappled extensively with the problem of MERS, resulting in New York being one of the only states to reject the right of MERS to foreclose as nominee for the lender by reason of the letter of the law. Under New York law, the right to foreclose is given to the actual Holder of both the note and mortgage, and not to the agent of the Holder. When the note is endorsed and delivered to MERS, then MERS can foreclose. But that is nothing new; any Holder of the note can foreclose. What is new is the refusal of the New York judicial system to accept the MERS model. New York does not accept MERS' standing to foreclose based on MERS being both mortgagee-in-title and/or nominee of the lender, because by law, the mortgagee does not have standing to foreclose without Holding the note. On a different level, New York finally accepted the right of MERS to assign the mortgage, after several high-profile cases denied MERS that right. New York should be given credit for seriously engaging the topic again and again in a seesaw of trial and error, mistakes and corrections, decisions, rejections and affirmations. (A third area of litigation – whether county clerk's must record MERS instruments is discussed in "MERS and the County Clerks")

The long saga of adjudication in New York begins pre-MERS with well-established case law holding that only the Holder of both the note and mortgage has standing to foreclose. Two typical cases that are often cited are *Kluge v. Fugazy* (145 AD 2d 537), which is pre-MERS, and *Katz v. Eastville Realty Co.* (249 AD2d 243) from 1998.

The waters were muddied early on by cases which were either improperly pled, or improperly reported. In *Mortgage Electronic Registration Systems, Inc. v. Burek* (4 Misc 3d 1030, 798 NYS2d 346) counsel for plaintiff claimed that MERS owns the note. As we have shown, MERS can never be the owner of the note; the MERS Membership Agreement actually forbids making that assertion. The judge didn't address this issue; the court simply denied summary judgment because of issues of fact. Another case with the same history is *Mortgage Electronic Registration Systems v. Bastian* (12 Misc 3ed 1182(A), 2006 WL 1985461) in which the judge mentions p. 3 "…that there is no evidence that (lender) ever assigned the note or mortgage to MERS." The impression was that MERS was shown not to have standing.

The first New York case to catch national attention with regards to MERS adjudication was *Lasalle Bank National Association v. Lamy* 2006 (NY Slip Op 51534 (U)[12 Misc 3d 1191(A)]). The judge starts off by citing *Kluge v. Fugazy* and *Katz v. Eastville Realty Co.* and incorrectly stating that p.2 "…only the owner of the note and mortgage at the time of the commencement of a foreclosure action may properly prosecute said action". It would have been more correct to use the word "holder" instead of "owner". This is pointed out in later cases such as *Silverberg* (see below). As explained in "MERS, Notes, and Mortgages", there is a difference between Holding and owning. (See Chapter 6 – Four Facets of Ownership of Notes). The court then further muddies the waters by stating that in *Mortgage Electronic Registration Systems, Inc. v. Burek* and *Mortgage Electronic Registration Systems v. Bastian*, MERS was denied standing because it was not the owner. First of all, it is not clear that either case actually made that determination. More importantly, if they did, they would have been wrong since owning the note is not the threshold criteria for standing in a foreclosure action (Holding the note is). Finally the judge in *LaSalle* determines that LaSalle Bank, as plaintiff, has no standing to foreclose because 1) the note was assigned to it at an indeterminable date (possibly after the complaint was filed which would indeed eliminate standing), and 2) MERS had no authority to assign the mortgage to LaSalle Bank. The judge writes that MERS p.5 "…had no ownership interest in either the note or the mortgage at the time the purported assignment thereof was made. The…assignment of mortgage is thus invalid". The judge clearly did not agree with the model presented in "MERS, Notes, and Mortgages", in which MERS holds title to the pledge of the collateral, but not the beneficial interest. In any case, this determination that MERS' assignments are invalid did not survive the New York court system.

A year later, in *Mortgage Electronic Registration Systems, Inc. v Coakley* (2007 NY Slip Op 05478[41 AD3d 674] the court clears up one of the mistakes regarding standing. The judge correctly states that the law grants standing to foreclose to the Holder of the note, not the owner. This corrects the mistaken assertion in *Lasalle Bank National Association v. Lamy* and brushes aside any mistaken interpretations arising from *Burek* and *Bastian*. In the *Coakley* case, the note was actually endorsed and delivered to MERS. (This was allowed up to July 22, 2011 and was done by a certified officer of the lender). As Holder of the note, and as mortgagee-in-title, MERS had standing to foreclose. On one hand, this was a powerful victory for MERS as it cleared up several issues and allowed them to foreclose. But it really was a hollow victory, because it gave MERS the right to fore-close only as Holder; but any Holder of the note can foreclose. In doing so, the court actually rejects MERS' claim that it can foreclose as nominee of the lender (i.e. without being the Holder of the note). Since the right to foreclose, as nominee for the lender was one rai-son d'etre for creating MERS, Coakley was really a defeat for MERS. Ironically, the judge mentions that by signing the mortgage docu-ment, the borrower gave MERS the power to foreclose: "Moreover, further support for MERS's standing to commence the action may be found on the face of the mortgage instrument itself. Pursuant to the clear and unequivocal terms of the mortgage instrument, Coak-ley expressly agreed without qualification that MERS had the right to foreclose...." Did this mean that the court would allow MERS to foreclose as nominee for the lender without being the holder? The answer turned out to be no. It took New York's highest court four years to clarify that.

In *Bank of New York v. Silverberg* the Appellate Court clarified that the only reason MERS could foreclose in *Coakley* was that MERS had been assigned the note. P.9 "In the absence of that crucial fact, the lan-guage in the mortgage instrument would not have provided 'further support' for the proposition that MERS had the power to foreclose in that case." The court clearly had not meant to imply in *Coakley* that MERS can foreclose as nominee for the lender. In *Silverberg*, the court repeatedly recites the law that in order to foreclose in New York, the plaintiff must be the Holder of the note and mortgage. Being nomi-nee of the holder isn't enough.

Silverberg is important since it closes the door on MERS foreclosing as nominee and closes any further debate on the issue. Unfortunately, the case is very confusing both because of the uncertainty as to the chain of events, and because the judges go off on an irrelevant tangent. The judges trip over themselves by discussing whether MERS can assign its right to foreclose. Mortgages with the MERS' boilerplate do not state that only MERS has the right to foreclose; rather, it leaves the door open for either the lender, or MERS, to foreclose. What MERS assigns is the title to the mortgage, not the rights that belong to the beneficial owner in any case. But the importance of the judge's ruling - that MERS cannot foreclose as nominee - transcends the judge's confusion as to the facts, and as to the mechanics of MERS, note and mortgages.

What about assignments of mortgage?

New York's court system is a little weird in that each of the 62 counties in New York State has a Supreme Court, which, in the event, is not supreme at all. They are really district level courts. Earlier we discussed the ruling in *LaSalle v. Lamy*, which was issued by the Supreme Court of Suffolk County. That court rejected MERS' authority to assign a mortgage. In early 2011, two other county Supreme Courts issued contrary rulings concerning MERS' right to assign mortgages. In *The Bank of New York v. Sameeh Alderazi* (2011 NY Slip Op 50547) the Supreme Court of Kings County held that MERS cannot assign the mortgage without explicit instructions of the lender; and since there was no proof that the lender (Countrywide in this case) instructed MERS to do so, the assignment is invalid. P. 3: "Plaintiff failed to provide any evidence that Countrywide had authorized MERS to assign its mortgage to Plaintiff." While the judge obviously is correct as to agency law, he does not seem to be aware of the mechanics of MERS operations. While there are millions of assignments signed by certified officers of MERS, not one is actually executed by MERS in

Virginia. As explained in the Tutorial, assignments are executed by employees of the respective lender, or servicer, or law firm handling the instruments. These employees are also certified to be "certified officers" of MERS, but they are never acting on MERS' instructions. They are acting on the instructions of their respective employers. A MERS assignment to Countrywide, is executed by an employee of Countrywide upon Countrywide's instructions. The fact that the Countrywide employee is called a certified officer of MERS, and the fact that the assignment purports to convey legal title to the mortgage from MERS to Countrywide, are legal fictions. But they are fictions that have become mainstay of the financial and legal worlds in all fifty states.

Concurrent with the *Alderazi* ruling, the Supreme Court of Bronx County decided that there's no problem with assignments executed by MERS. In *The Bank of New York Mellon Trust Company NA v. Eddie Sachar* (Index 380904/2009), the court simply recites the boilerplate found on every MERS mortgage giving MERS "legal title to the rights" granted by the mortgage document, and giving MERS the power to "take any action required of Lender". The court stated that there is no reason to think that the mortgage assignment executed by MERS was not done properly. And the final word goes to the Appellate Division of the New York Supreme Court which affirmed the ruling in May 2012.

This ebb and flow – first rejecting MERS' right to assign mortgage, and then accepting it – played out in the Federal Bankruptcy Court (Eastern District of New York) which ruled in the case *In re Agard* that a MERS assignment of mortgage was invalid in New York. The case garnered national attention and is very interesting to read, but is flawed. In this case, the lender requested relief from bankruptcy stay and the borrower challenged the lender's standing to request such relief. It took the judge only two pages to decide that the lender does indeed have standing to request relief from stay since, in this specific case, a state court had already issued a judgment for foreclosure. But then, the judge wrote out 35 pages to explain why MERS assignments are invalid in all other cases before the court.

1) The judge discusses the verbiage of the assignment of mortgage from MERS which declares that MERS assigns its interest in the mortgage and note to the plaintiff. The judge correctly points out that MERS does not have any interest in the note and can't assign it; but the judge incorrectly concludes that therefore the plaintiff does not Hold the note. This is the exact same mistake made in the *Bellistri* (Missouri). Millions of assignments-of-mortgage executed by MERS have this misleading verbiage. But that verbiage should not and cannot be used to disprove the chain of ownership of the note. The fact that MERS incorrectly declares that it is assigning the note to the plaintiff, does not mean that the plaintiff does not own, or Hold, the note. First of all, the plaintiff acquired its rights in the note from the previous owner, or from the previous Holder, and never from MERS. The MERS verbiage is meaningless. Secondly, the MERS' assignment of mortgage is never executed by MERS. It is always executed by an employee of the plaintiff (or by an employee of one of its agents) at the express order of the plaintiff. The plaintiff would not execute the assignment to itself unless it already had the note.

2) The decision also reviews the verbiage in the mortgage which empowers MERS as holder of legal title to the mortgage, and as nominee for the lender. Yet the court does not find this enough to empower MERS to assign the mortgage. Citing *LaSalle v. Lamy* and *Alderazi* (reviewed above), the court refuses to recognize MERS' right to assign the mortgage. The judge also repeats Prof. Peterson's mistaken

assertion that MERS cannot be mortgagee and agent of the mortgagee at the same time. As we have shown, MERS can be mortgagee-in –title, and agent for the mortgagee-in-equity at the same time.

In any case, this was a stunning exercise in overreach. Predictably, this case was overturned one year later as being "…an improper advisory opinion and should be vacated" (U.S. District Court Memorandum and Order 11-CV=1826(JS)). The appeals court explained that under Article 3 of the Constitution, a Federal Court cannot decide questions that do not affect the case in question. The end result was that MERS' power to assign mortgages is no longer challenged – in conformity with the Appellate Court's finding in *Sachar*.

An interesting defense of MERS' power to assign the mortgage can be found in an excellent case, *Deutsche Bank v. Pietranico* (2011 NY Slip Op 21261). The judge has two lines of argument. The first is historical: p. 15 "The concept of nominee appearing in the land records on behalf of the true owner has long been recognized. It has never been the case that the true owners of interests in real estate could be determined using land records". Secondly, the judge defends the right of the parties to a contract to define the terms of the contract: p. 21 "It is a fundamental principle that the courts should not interfere with the contractual rights set forth in a mortgage instrument". Then, referencing Alderazi and Agard, the judge turns very critical: p. 17 "…what is unusual is the extent various courts will go to limit the contractual role of MERS as a nominee". The judge also criticizes Kansas case *Landmark v. Kesler* reviewed above. That case states: "..a nominee possess few or no legally enforceable rights beyond those of a principal whom the nominee serves". The judge of Pietranico replies: "..where is the suggestion that MERS, as a "common agent" is enforcing rights **beyond** those of a principal" (highlighting is mine).

Another interesting angle in Pietranico is the judges' implication that, while the plaintiff must Hold the note at the time the complaint is filed, the mortgage can be assigned afterward. While many states would agree, I'm not sure that New York law would tolerate that scenario. In any case, *Pietranico* is an excellent case to read because of all of these topics.

Summary:

1) **Assignments of Mortgage**: While early cases such as *Lamy*, *Alderazi* and *Agard* refused to recognize the legitimacy of MERS' assignments of mortgage, the Appellate Court eventually recognized MERS' right and power to assign mortgages, by reversing *Agard*, and affirming *Sachar*.

2) **MERS as Plaintiff in Foreclosure as Nominee of the Lender**: New York, like Maine and Vermont, was one of the few states to deny MERS' standing to foreclose as nominee of the lender, based on the letter of law demanding that the plaintiff hold both the note and mortgage. This comes through in *Coakley* as clarified by *Silverberg*. Agency does not suffice in New York.

So three states – New York, Vermont, and Maine did not allow MERS to be the plaintiff in a foreclosure case when it acted as agent ("nominee") for the lender. Two final points on this matter:

1) It is interesting to note that these three states are Lien-Theory States. As explained above, Lien-Theory states are very strict as to the requirement of possessing the note on the date the complaint is filed. These three states went one step further and demanded that the Holder, and not the agent of the holder, initiate the process. Title-Theory states do not have

this requirement and no Title-Theory state denied MERS' right to be plaintiff while this litigation was in play.

2) I believe that none of these three states would object to MERS being the plaintiff if MERS were Holder of the note. The mechanism, by which MERS became Holder, is explained in the Chapter V.2.b. above. The end result though, is that MERS' capacity to be plaintiff – either as agent or as Holder - was recognized in every state that the issue was litigated. MERS won every battle in which it was engaged. And as explained above, it surrendered on July 22, 2011.

APPENDIX C:

CITATIONS OF CASES

Alabama
Crum v. LaSalle Bank, N.A., 55 So.3d 266 (Ala. Civ. App. 2009).
Henderson v. Merscorp., Inc., No. 1091716 (Ala. Sept. 9, 2011).
*Lexis Cite: Henderson v. Merscorp, Inc., 2011 Ala. LEXIS 597 (Ala. Sept. 9, 2011).

Arizona
Cervantes v. Countrywide Home Loans, Inc., 656 F.3d 1034 (9th Cir. 2011).
Ciardi v. Lending Co., Inc., No. CV 10-0275-PHX-JAT (U.S. District Court, D. Arizona 2010).
*Lexis Cite: Ciardi v. The Lending Co., 2010 U.S. Dist. LEXIS 50878 (D. Ariz. May 24, 2010).

Arkansas
Mortg. Elec. Registration Sys., Inc. v. S.W. Homes of Ark., 301 S.W. 3d 1(Ark. 2009).
Coley v. Accredited Home Lenders, Inc., No. 4:10CV01870 JLH (E.D. Ark. Jan. 3, 2011).

California
*Lexis Cite: Sulak v. Mortg. Elec. Registration Sys., Inc., 2006 Cal. App. Unpub. LEXIS 11045 (Cal. App. 4th Dist. Dec. 7, 2006).
*WestLaw Cite: Sulak v. Mortg. Elec. Registration Sys., Inc., E038916, 2006 WL 3514873 (Cal. App. 4th Dist. 2006).
Gomes v. Countrywide Home Loans, Inc., 192 Cal. App. 4th 1149 (Cal. App. 4th Dist. 2011).

Ferguson v. Avelo Mortg., 126 Cal. Rptr. 3d 586 (Cal. App. 2d Dist. 2011), as modified (June 20, 2011).

Connecticut
*Lexis Cite: Mortg. Elec. Registration Sys., Inc. v. Ventura, 2006 Conn. Super, LEXIS 1154 (Conn. Super. Ct. Apr. 20, 2006).
*Westlaw Cite: Mortgage Electronic Registration Systems, Inc. v. Ventura, CV054003168S, 2006 WL 1230265 (Conn. Super. 2006).

Florida
Mortg. Elec. Registration Sys., Inc. v. Azize, 965 So. 2d 151 (Fla. 2d Dist. App. 2007).
Mortg. Elec. Registration Sys., Inc. v. Revoredo, 955 So. 2d 33 (Fla. 3d Dist. App. 2007).
Trent v. Mortg. Elec. Registration Sys. Inc., 288 Fed. Appx. 571 (11th Cir. Fla. 2008).
Taylor v. Deutsche Bank Nat. Trust Co., 44 So. 3d 618 (Fla. 5th Dist. App. 2010).

Georgia
Drake v. Citizens Bank (In re Corley), 447 B.R. 375 (Bankr. S.D. Ga. 2011).

Hawaii
Countrywide Home Loans, Inc. v. Wilkerson (In re O'Kelley), 420 B.R. 18 (D. Haw. 2009).

Idaho
In re Sheridan, No. 08-20381-TLM (Bankr. D. Idaho Mar. 12, 2009).
*Lexis Cite: In re Sheridan, 2009 Bankr. LEXIS 552 (Bankr. D. Idaho Mar. 12, 2009).
In re Wilhelm, 407 B.R. 392 (Bankr. D. Idaho 2009).
Trotter v. Bank of New York Mellon, 275 P.3d 857 (Idaho 2012).

Illinois
Mortg. Elec. Registration Sys., Inc. v. Barnes, 940 N.E.2d 118 (Ill. App. 1st Dist. 2010).

Indiana
Citimortgage, Inc. v. Barabas, 975 N.E.2d 805, 809 (Ind. 2012).

Kansas
Mortg. Elec. Registration Sys., Inc. v. Graham, 247 P.3d 223 (Kan. App. 2010).
Landmark Nat. Bank v. Kesler, 216 P.3d 158 (Kan. 2009).
In re Martinez, 444 B.R. 192 (Bankr. D. Kan. 2011) clarified on denial of reconsideration, 455 B.R. 755 (Bankr. D. Kan. 2011).

Kentucky
Deutsche Bank Nat'l Trust Co. v. Moody, No. 09-CI-4463 (Fayette Circuit Court Fourth Division Apr. 11, 2011).

Maine
Mortg. Elec. Registration Sys., Inc. v. Saunders, 2 A.3d 289 (Me. 2010).

Maryland
Suss v. JP Morgan Chase Bank, No. WMN-09-1627 (D. Md. July 9, 2010).
Lexis Cite: Suss v. JP Morgan Chase Bank, 2010 U.S. Dist. LEXIS 68777 (D. Md. July 9, 2010).

Massachusetts
In re Huggins, 357 B.R. 180 (Bankr. D. Mass. 2006).
In re Lopez, 446 B.R. 12, 18 (Bankr. D. Mass. 2011).

Michigan
Residential Funding Co. v. Saurman, 807 N.W.2d 412 (Mich. App. 2011).
Knox v. Trott & Trott, P.C., No. 10-13175 (E.D. Mich. Apr. 21, 2011).

*Lexis Cite: Knox v. Trott & Trott, P.C., 2011 U.S. Dist. LEXIS 43311 (E.D. Mich. Apr. 21, 2011).
Residential Funding Co. v. Saurman, 805 N.W.2d 183 (Mich. 2011).

Minnesota
Jackson v. Mortg. Elec. Registration Sys., Inc., 770 N.W.2d 487 (Minn. 2009).

Missouri
Bellistri v. Ocwen Loan Servicing, L.L.C., 284 S.W.3d 619, 623 (Mo. App. E. Dist. 2009).
Mortgage Elec. Registration Sys. v. Bellistri, No. 4:09-CV-731 CAS (E.D. Mo. July 1, 2010).
*Lexis Cite: Mortgage Elec. Registration Sys. v. Bellistri, 2010 U.S. Dist. LEXIS 67753 (E.D. Mo. July 1, 2010).

Montana
Waide v. U.S. Bank Nat'l Assn., No. DV 10-1763 (Montana Thirteenth Judicial District Court June 28, 2011).

Nebraska
Mortg. Elec. Registration Sys., Inc. v. Nebraska Dept. of Banking and Fin., 704 N.W.2d 784 (Neb. 2005).

Nevada
*Lexis Cite: In re Mitchell, 2009 Bankr. LEXIS 876 (Bankr. D. Nev. Mar. 31, 2009).
*WestLaw Cite: In re Mitchell, BK-S-07-16226-LBR, 2009 WL 1044368 (Bankr. D. Nev. 2009) *aff'd on other grounds*, 423 B.R. 914 (D. Nev. 2009).
Mortgage Electronic Registration Systems, Inc. v. Chong, No. 2:09-CV-00661-KJD-LRL (D. Nev. Dec. 4, 2009).
Smith v. Community Lending, Inc., 773 F. Supp. 2d 941 (D. Nev. 2011).

New Hampshire
Powers v. Aurora Loan Services, No. 213-2010-CV-00181 (N.H. Super. Ct. 2011).
*Lexis Cite: Powers v. Aurora Loan Servs., 2011 N.H. Super. LEXIS 50 (N.H. Super. Ct. 2011).

New Jersey
Bank of New York v. Raftogianis, 13 A.3d 435 (N.J. Super. Ch. Div. 2010).

New York
MERSCORP, Inc. v. Romaine, 861 N.E.2d 81 (N.Y. 2006).
Bank of N.Y. Mellon Trust Co. v. Sachar, 943 N.Y.S.2d 893 (N.Y. App. Div. 1st Dept. 2012).
In re Agard, 444 B.R. 231 (Bankr. E.D.N.Y. 2011) vacated in part sub nom.
*Westlaw Cite: Agard v. Select Portfolio Servicing, Inc., BR 8-10-77338 REG, 2012 WL 1043690 (E.D.N.Y. 2012).
*Lexis Cite: Agard v. Select Portfolio Servicing, Inc., 2012 U.S. Dist. LEXIS 43286 (E.D.N.Y. Mar. 28, 2012).
Mortg. Elec. Registration Sys., Inc. v. Coakley, 838 N.Y.S.2d 622 (N.Y. App. Div. 2d Dept. 2007).
Bank of N. Y. v. Silverberg, 926 N.Y.S.2d 532 (N.Y. App. Div. 2d Dept. 2011).
Deutsche Bank Nat. Trust Co. v. Pietranico, 928 N.Y.S.2d 818 (N.Y. Sup. Ct. 2011) *aff'd,* 957 N.Y.S.2d 868 (N.Y. App. Div. 2d Dept. 2013).

North Dakota
Bray v. Bank of America, No. 1:09-CV-075 (D. N.D. Jan. 5, 2011).
*Westlaw Cite: Bray v. Bank of Am., 1:09-CV-075, 2011 WL 30307 (D.N.D. 2011) *appeal dismissed,* 435 Fed. Appx. 571 (8th Cir. 2011) (unpublished) and *aff'd,* 497 Fed. Appx. 685 (8th Cir. 2013) (unpublished).

Ohio
Mortg. Elec. Registration Sys., Inc. v. Mosley, 2010-Ohio-2886 (Ohio App. 8th Dist. 2010).

Oklahoma
Mortgage Electronic Registration System, Inc. v. Warden, No. CJ-2005-7027 (District Court of Oklahoma Cty. March 3, 2006).

Oregon
Rinegard-Guirma v. Bank of America, No. 10-1065-PK (D. Or. Oct. 6, 2010).
In re Allman, 2010 WL 3366405 (Bankr. D. Or. Oct. 20, 2011).
Bertrand v. Suntrust Mortg., Inc., No. 09-857-JO (D. Or. Mar. 23, 2011).
*Lexis Cite: Bertrand v. SunTrust Mortg., Inc., 2011 U.S. Dist. LEXIS 31442 (D. Or. Mar. 23, 2011).
Spencer v. Guaranty Bank, No. 10CV0515ST (Circuit Court of the State of Oregon – County of Deschutes, May 5, 2011).
Hooker v. Northwest Tr. Servs., No. 10-3111-PA (D. Or. May 25, 2011).
*Lexis Cite: Hooker v. Northwest Tr. Servs., 2011 U.S. Dist. LEXIS 57005 (D. Or. May 25, 2011).
Buckland v. Aurora Loan Services, No. 10 CV 1023 (Circuit Court Oregon March 18, 2011).

Pennsylvania
Mortg. Elec. Registration Sys., Inc. v. Estate of Watson, No. 637 (Superior Court of Pennsylvania WDA 2006, filed December 27, 2006).
Mortg. Elec. Registration Sys., Inc. v. Ralich, 982 A.2d 77 (Pa. Super. 2009).

Rhode Island
Bucci v. Lehman Brothers Bank, 68 A.3d 1069 (R.I. 2013).

Texas

Athey v. Mortg. Elec. Registration Systems, Inc., 314 S.W.3d 161 (Tex. App. Eastland 2010).

Knighton v. Merscorp Inc., 304 Fed. Appx. 285 (5th Cir. 2008) (unpublished).

Utah

Wade v. Meridias Capital, Inc., No. 2:10CV998 DS (D. Utah Mar. 17, 2011).

*Lexis Cite: Wade v. Meridias Capital, Inc., U.S. Dist. LEXIS 28414 (D. Utah Mar. 17, 2011).

Wareing v. Meridias Capital, Inc., No. 2:10-CV-165 TS (D. Utah Mar. 17, 2011).

*Lexis Cite: Wareing v. Meridias Capital, Inc., 2011 U.S. Dist. LEXIS 28410 (D. Utah Mar. 17, 2011).

Marty v. Mortg. Elec. Registration Sys., Inc., No. 1:10-cv-00033-CW (D. Utah Oct. 19, 2010).

*Lexis Cite: Marty v. Mortg. Elec. Registration Sys., Inc., 2010 U.S. Dist. LEXIS 111209 (D. Utah Oct. 19, 2010).

Vermont

Mortg. Elec. Registration Sys., Inc. v. Johnston, No. 420-6-09 Rdcv (Vt. Super. Ct. Oct. 28, 2009).

*Lexis Cite: Mortg. Elec. Registration Sys., Inc. v. Johnston, 2009 Vt. Super. LEXIS 15 (Vt. Super. Ct. Oct. 28, 2009).

CitiMortgage v. Bischoff, No. 255-4-09 Rdcv (Vt. Super. Ct. Oct. 28, 2009).

*Lexis Cite: CitiMortgage, Inc. v. Bischoff, 2009 Vt. Super. LEXIS 2 (Vt. Super. Ct. Oct. 28, 2009).

Virginia

Graves v. Mortg. Elec. Registration Sys., Inc., No. CL-2010-17101 (19th Judicial Circuit of Virginia June 29, 2011).

Washington

Bain v. Metro. Mortg. Group, Inc., 285 P.3d 34 (Wash. 2012). Available on WestlawNext.

Vawter v. Quality Loan Service Corp., 707 F.Supp.2d 1115 (W.D. Wash. 2010).

West Virginia

Wittenberg v. First Indep. Mortg. Co., No. 3:10-CV-58 (N.D. W. Va. Apr. 11, 2011).

*Lexis Cite: Wittenberg v. First Indep. Mortg. Co., 2011 U.S. Dist. LEXIS 39310 (N.D. W. Va. Apr. 11, 2011).

Wisconsin

Mortg. Elec. Registration Sys., Inc. v. Degner, No. 05CV1982 (Circuit Court of Waukesha County)(unpublished).

Wyoming

In re Martinez, No. 09-21124 (Bankr. D. Wyo. Mar. 16, 2011).

*Lexis Cite: In re Martinez, 2011 Bankr. LEXIS 982 (Bankr. D. Wyo. Mar. 16, 2011).